MW01489989

INSTANT POT COOKBOOK

1000 Day Delicious, Quick & Easy Instant Pot Recipes for Beginners and Advanced Users

By

ROBERT JONES

© Copyright 2021 by Robert Jones – All rights reserved.

All rights reserved. No part of this publication or the information in it may be quoted from or reproduced in any form by means such as printing, scanning, photocopying or otherwise without prior written permission of the copyright holder.

Disclaimer and Terms of Use:

Effort has been made to ensure that the information in this book is accurate and complete, however, the author and the publisher do not warrant the accuracy of the information, text and graphics contained within the book due to the rapidly changing nature of science, research, known and unknown facts and internet. The Author and the publisher do not hold any responsibility for errors, omissions or contrary interpretation of the subject matter herein. This book is presented solely for motivational and informational purposes only.

TABLE OF CONTENTS

SOUPS AND STEWS

INTRODUCTION

Welcome to the exciting and a little wild world of Instant Pots, the multi-tasking kitchen appliances designed to make people's life a whole lot easier. The instant pot has recently become a popular brand that has a bunch of pre-programmed settings to reduce the work of cooks. An instant pot is a sauté pan, a yogurt maker, a rice cooker, a steamer and an electric pressure cooker. It is a wonderful kitchen appliance that will give you freedom and more options because it will enable you to prepare different meals in less time. You can cook everything from hard-boiled eggs and stews to very simple soup recipes with an instant pot.

It's very easy to cook with an instant pot. You just need to add the ingredients and some liquid to the pot, choose the cooking program on the recipe, then wait until the timer is done and lastly, release the pressure and enjoy your meal. Therefore, pressure cooking is super easy because you just need to press a button to reach high pressure and then turn a valve to release it.

Pressure cooking has several merits such as it's healthy, simple, clean, fast, and safe. An instant pot cooks contents at a higher temperature and pressure compared to other conventional cooking. This means that the food cooks faster within a short period of time. According to a research done food experts, it was discovered that pressure cooking is healthy because about ninety percent of the vitamins and minerals are preserved compared to boiling, which preserves about forty percent. Therefore, it's best if you steam your fruits and vegetables to preserve the taste, texture and vitamins. Most pressure cookers require less energy to operate the cooking cycle. This means that you will increase your energy savings compared to conventional cooking. The recent pressure cookers such as instant pots come with safety mechanisms that prevent hazards from occurring.

The instant pot was first introduced in late 2010 by a team of technology veterans from Canada. Their main drive was to find solutions that would help busy families to make quality food in the shortest time possible, promote healthy eating and reduce the consumption of fast foods. The team finally created an instant pot that was a pressure cooker, rice cooker, steamer, warmer, and slow cooker. Since then, there has been new developments to make versatile products to meet customer demands. You can buy an instant pot on Amazon, or any other trusted seller.

What's an Instant Pot?

An instant pot is a programmable electric multi-cooker that is designed to quickly cook foods at high pressure. The pressure of steam usually builds up inside the pot thereby increasing the temperature that speeds up the cooking process. The instant pot is safer and even easier to use compared to the old pressure cookers because the pot comes with many safety features. The instant pot is a popular multi-cooker and has lots of functions such as slow cooking, steaming, rice cooking, pressure cooking, sautéing and warming. The pot is very versatile and you will love the texture and flavor of foods when you cook with it. The pressure created in your instant pot can tenderize any tough meat you have and a nice way to have better chili. There are different models of instant pots with sizes ranging from three-quart to 8 quarts. Some examples of instant pot models are the Instant Pot Duo Plus, Instant Pot Duo, Instant Pot Smart Bluetooth, Instant Pot Ultra and Instant Pot Lux.

In the past, there were safety issues with pressure cookers which would make them seem dangerous. For this reason, many people would avoid using pressure cookers in their kitchen and would prefer other methods of cooking. This lead to the introduction of instant pots that were regarded as safer and easier to use. The instant pot comprises of a lid, a stainless steel inner pot and an outer base all of which have in-built safety mechanisms. According to kitchen appliance experts, the instant pot has a silicone gasket that is responsible for preventing steam from escaping and this greatly helps in regulating pressure. Therefore, in case your gasket is ruined or damaged, the best thing you should do is replace it immediately.

Here are lists of parts and accessories to expect if you have just bought an instant pot. Open the pot by turning the lid in an anticlockwise direction and then lift it. To close it, just turn the lid in a clockwise direction. Remove plastic wrap from the accessories and the stainless inner pot. Below are parts and accessories you will find:

- Instant pot's lid. The design of the lid varies between models.
- The base unit which the outer covering and has a heating element attached to it at the bottom.
- Power cord which is removable or non-removable depending on your model.
- Inner pot made of stainless steel. This pot usually fits perfectly into the base unit.
- Trivet. Use the trivet to raise foods inside the pot. It will help you separate foods from liquids, for example, when cooking hard-boiled eggs.
- Steam release valve. It is located on top of the lid and helps in releasing pressure.
- Condensation collector. This is usually attached to the back of an instant pot. However, some models don't have a condensation collector.

Wash all the parts and accessories of your pot before you can start using it. Some accessories are dishwasher safe like the inner pot, lid and the steam valve but you can wash with hands if you like. For the base unit, just wash with hands and never submerge in water.

Instant Pot Safety Tips and Cleaning

1. The Two Most Important Safety Instructions for Your Instant Pot

All instant pots come with a manual that contains information such as important safeguards, product information, care and maintenance, controls and states of the cooker, troubleshooting and many more. If this is your first time to use an instant pot, it is recommended to first read the manual carefully to better understand how the pot functions and the precautions to observe. Furthermore, you should keep the manual in a safe place for future reference in case you have troubles with your instant pot.

The following are the most important safety instructions you should adhere to when operating your instant pot:

- Never at any point put your face close to the float valve or the steam release valve when the instant pot is switched on. Always face away when opening the lid to avoid burning your skin. After the cooking cycle is done and you want to release the pressure by turning the steam valve to the venting position, you should use the handle of a long spoon to do that. Do not use your hand to prevent chances of being burnt by the hot steam escaping from the valve opening. Alternatively, you should use any kitchen utensil that has a long handle or use the oven mitt to gently move the steam valve.
- Secondly, do not open the lid when your instant pot is still pressurized. First, allow the pressure to be released and then open the lid. To know whether all pressure has been released inside the pot, check if the float valve has dropped down. The float valve may be silver or red in color depending on your model. In some models, the silver float valve moves up to be at the same level with the lid when the instant pot is pressurized and below the lid level when not pressurized. In some cases, the red float valve pops up above the lid level when your pot is under pressure. Make sure you read your manual carefully to better understand your instant pot's float valve.

2. What You Should Inspect In Your Instant Pot Before Each Use

- Check the base of your instant pot but you will have to first remove the inner pot. On the base, you will find a heating element. Before using your instant pot, make sure the heating element is dry and there is no debris present. After you wash the stainless inner pot, make sure you dry it thoroughly before installing back it onto the base of your instant pot.
- Check to ascertain that the silicone sealing ring on the lid is properly fitted. It should also be clean and free from damage.
- Inspect your instant pot's steam release valve before cooking. Carefully pull the steam valve straight upwards to remove it from the pot. Ensure there is no food debris and it's clean. There are foods that foam and froth when cooking them such as rice and pasta and they can clog onto the steam valve. In case the steam valve is clogged, clean it with running water and then install it back onto the pot.
- Another checkup you need to look at is the float valve on your instant pot. The float valve is located close to the steam release valve. Make sure the float valve is clean and no visible debris in it. If there is food debris inside the float valve, use warm water to clean or put the lid under clean running water to clean it.

Instant Pot Water Test

Once you buy an instant pot for the first time, it's recommended that you complete a water test before you start cooking with it. Make sure that you follow the instructions on the manual so that you can understand how pressure cooking works. A water test is important because it ensures the instant pot is functioning properly and will help you be comfortable with the pressure cooker.

Follow these steps of water test

1. Connect the power cable to the instant pot firmly and then plug it to a power socket.
2. Put the inner pot which is made of stainless steel in the base and then add three cups of potable water.
3. Check the instant pot lid to make sure that the silicone ring is properly fitted. Cover the instant pot with its lid and turn until it is at the closed position. In case the instant pot is connected to a power supply, it will chime every time you open and close the lid.
4. Move steam release nozzle to the seal position. If using an instant pot ultra, the steam valve will automatically move to the seal position once you close the lid.
5. Push the pressure cook or manual button. You will notice that some models of instant pots have a button that reads pressure cook or manual button.
6. Set the timer to five minutes and then wait for the instant pot to start the cycle.
7. The pot will probably take about five to fifteen minutes to reach pressure. When the pot reaches high pressure, the steam valve will pop out and then the timer will start counting from five minutes. As pressure builds up, you may hear some hissing sounds and even notice the escape of steam from the steam nozzle. Besides, you might note a plastic smell the very first time when using the instant pot. This happens only once and you shouldn't smell plastic ever again.
8. You will hear beep sounds from the instant pot once the five minutes elapse. The pot will then change to keep warm function and the timer will begin counting up minutes. At this time, the cooking cycle is done.
9. To perform the water test, you will need to do a quick release so that you can release the pressure inside the instant pot. Do a quick release by gently moving the steam release nozzle to the vent position. You can use a long spoon to flip the steam valve to avoid being burnt by the hot steam escaping from the nozzle.
10. Once the steam valve drops down and pressure has been released, remove the lid. You can now start cooking your favorite foods with the new instant pot.

Note that in case the water test fails and the instant pot does not reach high pressure, make sure that the steam valve is moved to the seal position when performing the test. Also, make sure that the sealing ring on the lid is properly fitted. If you have done everything correctly and still have problems doing the water test, you should contact the manufacturer for further assistance.

How to Use the Instant Pot

You will need to know a few simple things when using the instant pot. It is simple to understand how an instant pot functions and every model has its own unique buttons that are labeled differently. Therefore, check the manual that comes with the instant pot.

Below are things you should know:

1. The minimum liquid required: In general, instant pots use steam and high pressure to cook all kinds of food and in order to create steam and pressure, you will need some liquid. Therefore, you will need at least one cup of liquid whenever you want to cook in an instant pot. Some recipes will require more liquid while others will need less liquid. Make sure you follow the instructions on recipes from genuine sources to avoid burning of food.

2. The maximum fill level: The inner pot of an instant pot has a line mark for 2/3 and ½. Do not at any one point fill the pot with liquid or food higher than the 2/3 line mark prior to cooking. If cooking something that will probably expand when cooking such as beans or rice, never fill the inner pot higher than the ½ line mark.

3. The manual/pressure cook button: There are different brands of instant pots and the pressure cook button is labeled differently. Some models label it 'pressure cook' while others label it 'manual'. This is the button you push to begin pressure cooking. The timer is set by pressing the + / - buttons.

4. The sauté button: press this button if you want to sauté your food in the instant pot. This function is great because it eliminates the need for using a separate pot on your stove. This means that you can brown and sauté your food in the instant pot. Never at any point put the inner pot over the stove. Make use of the sauté function to thicken the sauces once you pressure cook. Another important thing to note is never sauté while the pot is covered with the lid. The default time is set 30 minutes when you press sauté button but switch it off when you like by pushing cancel.

5. The cancel/keep warm button: Press this button to switch on/off the keep warm mode or stop the cooking process. Note that once the cooking cycle is done, the pot will automatically change to keep warm function.

6. The program buttons: All instant pot models have program options such as slow cook, steam, yogurt, multigrain, rice, porridge, egg, stew/meat, chili/bean, and broth/soup. All these program modes have their own pre-set times for cooking but you can adjust the cook times as you like. You don't have to use the pre-set cook times.

7. The pressure button: This button is also labeled as pressure level in some models. Use this button to set the pressure either high or low. However, most of the instant pot recipes you will come across will require cooking at high pressure. If you are using the instant pot LUX series, you can only cook at high-pressure setting because it lacks the pressure button.

8. The adjust button: Use this key to set to either High, Normal and Less cooking functions. The adjust button is essential especially if using the sauté function because you can control the heat level inside your instant pot.

9. How to use the trivet: All instant pot models come with a metal trivet that you should use in case you want to raise your food to keep it from touching the pot's bottom. Use the metal trivet to separate certain foods from the liquid on the base of your instant pot or keep away from direct heat on the pot's bottom. For example, you will want to use a trivet when baking potatoes or cooking hard-boiled eggs.

10. Covering the instant pot with lid: Your instant pot base has a track on the back upper edge. Lift the lid by its handle, then fit it on using the track and turn clockwise to close

the lid. Ensure the arrow in front of the lid lines up with arrow close to the locked sign at the base unit. In case the instant pot is on, you should hear a chime sound after closing the lid.

11. How to seal the pot: Seal your instant pot by moving the steam release nozzle to the sealing spot. You will notice that the steam valve a little unsteady and fits loosely. You will have to move the steam valve to the sealing spot each time you want to pressure cook in an instant pot.

12. Total time versus cook time: You should probably know that the cooking cycle takes is longer compared to the real cooking time of a certain recipe. An instant pot takes a few minutes to reach cooking pressure before cooking time can begin. Normally, it takes approximately ten minutes but the time varies with the temperature of food and liquid in your pot, the amount and type of food and the size of your pot. In addition, you will need to consider the time required to pressure release once the cooking cycle ends.

13. Performing a quick release: This is done manually to force out pressure from an instant pot. You just need to turn the steam from the seal position to the vent position to release the pressure inside the pot. Be careful when turning the steam valve to the vent position because the steam will immediately start to escape and can burn you. Keep off your face from the venting position. You can use a long spoon to turn the valve to avoid burning your hand. A quick-release is important if you want to stop food from cooking and this helps to prevent overcooking.

14. Natural pressure release: This is whereby you allow the pressure inside an instant pot to be released naturally by leaving the pot to rest once the cooking cycles has ended. Natural release often takes about ten to twenty minutes. It is important to perform a natural pressure release if the pot is full especially when cooking foamy foods, to prevent hot foam from oozing out of the steam valve.

15. Removing the lid safely: Never try to remove the lid from the instant pot when the pot is under high pressure inside. You should instead wait until all the pressure is released and this is indicated when the steam valve has dropped down. Once the steam release valve has dropped, grasp the lid's handle, then turn it anticlockwise and then gently lift it.

What to Expect From This Cookbook

This is a cookbook with recipes that are all cooked in an instant pot. The cookbook will give you all the knowledge that you require to begin using your instant pot. You will learn how to use each of the instant pot cooking function from the book's introduction. The recipes are simple and easy to understand and they clearly indicate the cooking times and even the pressure levels. This book will help you learn about instant pots, the safety tips, how to use an instant pot, features of an instant pot, inspecting your instant pot before each use, how to do a water test in a new instant pot and how to clean the parts and accessories of an instant pot.

The recipes in this cookbook are healthy and family-friendly meals for breakfast, lunch and dinner and some are even kid-friendly. Plus, some recipes are ready in about ten minutes.

Furthermore, there are options for paleo-friendly, vegan and gluten-free lifestyles. Maintaining a healthy life can be challenging but lifestyle changes such as eating healthy foods and engaging in physical activities can greatly help reduce your risk for heart-related diseases and other conditions.

The recipes have been grouped into different categories, five categories to be specific. They include eggs and vegetables, soups and stews, seafood and poultry, beef and pork and lastly, desserts.

All the recipes in this cookbook have a certain order to make them look neat and nice. You will find this order in all recipes:

- The title of the recipe.
- A clear picture of the recipe.
- The meal preparation time, actual cooking time and total servings.
- The ingredients of the recipe.
- Step by step instructions on how to prepare the recipe.
- Cooking tips in some of the recipes.

MEASUREMENT CONVERSIONS

US Dry Volume Measurements

1/16 teaspoon	Dash
1/8 teaspoon	Pinch
3 teaspoons	1 tablespoon
1/8 cup	2 tablespoons (1 standard coffee scoop)
1/4 cup	4 tablespoons
1/3 cup	5 tablespoons plus 1 teaspoon
1/2 cup	8 tablespoons
3/4 cup	12 tablespoons
1 cup	16 tablespoons
1 pound	16 ounces

US Liquid Volume Measurements

8 Fluid ounces	1 Cup
1 Pint	2 Cups (16 fluid ounces)
1 Quart	2 Pints (4 cups)
1 Gallon	4 Quarts (16 cups)

US to Metric Conversions

1/5 teaspoon	1 ml (ml stands for milliliter, one thousandth of a liter)
1 teaspoon	5 ml
1 tablespoon	15 ml
1 fluid oz.	30 ml
1/5 cup	50 ml
1 cup	240 ml
2 cups (1 pint)	470 ml
4 cups (1 quart)	.95 liter
4 quarts (1 gal)	3.8 liters
1 oz.	28 grams
1 pound	454 grams

Metric to US Conversions

1 milliliter	1/5 teaspoon
5 ml	1 teaspoon
15 ml	1 tablespoon
30 ml	1 fluid oz.
100 ml	3.4 fluid oz.
240 ml	1 cup
1 liter	34 fluid oz.
1 liter	4.2 cups
1 liter	2.1 pints
1 liter	1.06 quarts
1 liter	.26 gallon
1 gram	.035 ounce
100 grams	3.5 ounces
500 grams	1.10 pounds
1 kilogram	2.205 pounds
1 kilogram	35 oz.

Temperature Conversions

Fahrenheit	Celsius	Gas Mark
275° F	140° C	gas mark 1 - cool
300° F	150° C	gas mark 2
325° F	165° C	gas mark 3 - very moderate
350° F	180° C	gas mark 4 - moderate
375° F	190° C	gas mark 5
400° F	200° C	gas mark 6-moderately hot
425° F	220° C	gas mark 7 - hot
450° F	230° C	gas mark 9
475° F	240° C	gas mark 10 - very hot

Abbreviations

Cooking Abbreviation(s)	Unit of Measurement
C, c	cup
g	gram
kg	kilogram
L, l	liter
lb	pound
mL, ml	milliliter
oz	ounce
pt	pint
t, tsp	teaspoon
T, TB, Tbl, Tbsp	tablespoon

INSTANT POT RECIPES

SEAFOOD AND POULTRY

1. INSTANT POT LEMON OLIVE GREEK CHICKEN

Preparation Time: 15 minutes | Cooking Time: 17 to 19 minutes | Serves: 1

Ingredients

For marinating chicken:

- 2 tablespoon honey
- 8 chicken thighs, boneless and skinless
- 3 cloves garlic, fresh and minced
- ½ teaspoon smoked paprika
- 2 tablespoons olive oil
- ½ teaspoon garlic powder
- Juice from 1 lemon
- 1 tablespoon Greek Seasoning
- Pepper and salt to taste

For the sauce:

- 1 tablespoon water for slurry
- 1 whole lemon juice
- 1 tablespoon cornstarch for slurry
- Chopped fresh rosemary for garnish
- ¼ cup cream

On the day of cooking:

- ½ cup chicken broth
- 3 tablespoons butter
- ½ cup pitted Kalamata Olives

- 1 small chopped onion
- Zest of half a lemon, if desired

Instructions

1. Into a large ziplock bag, place the chicken thighs and then add honey, all seasonings, lemon juice, and olive oil. Seal the bag and then squeeze to coat all the thighs well.

2. Place Kalamata olives and chopped onions in a separate small bag.

3. On the day of cooking, set the instant pot to sauté on low and then place in olives, chopped onions, and butter. Let to cook for 1 to 2 minutes until just starting to soften. Place a single layer of chicken thighs and then sear on both sides for about 3 to 4 minutes. Transfer the cooked chicken to a plate until all the thighs are cooked.

4. Once all the chicken thighs are seared, place back the meat along with juice into the instant pot. Add in the lemon juice to de-glaze the pan. Add in chicken broth and then cover with the lid. Seal the steaming valve and then set to cook for 7 minutes on high pressure. Leave the chicken to rest for 3 minutes on no pressure release. Then open the valve carefully and quick release the remaining pressure.

5. Transfer the olives, onions and chicken onto a platter and leave the juices inside the instant pot. Switch to medium sauté, and pour in cream. Heat to a low boil, and mix in the water/cornstarch slurry. Place the chicken back into the pot and cook for about 3 minutes until the sauce has attained the desired consistency.

2. BUFFALO CHICKEN TORTILLA PIE IN THE INSTANT POT

Preparation Time: 15 minutes | Cooking Time: 35 minutes | Serves: 1

Ingredients

- 1 carrot
- 1 ½ Ibs. Chicken breast
- 2 stalks celery
- 5 flour tortilla shells
- Celery salt or seed to suit your taste
- Blue cheese dressing
- Sharp cheddar cheese
- 1 cup Buffalo Chicken wing sauce (you can use Ken's brand)
- Blue cheese

Instructions

1. Pour a cup of water into the instant pot. Add chicken breast and let it cook for 15 minutes on high pressure with a natural release. Take the chicken and water from the pot once done.

2. Place the cooked chicken, buffalo sauce, celery salt, chicken wing and chopped celery in a separate bowl. Shred the chicken thoroughly with a mixer or fork. Use non-stick cooking spray to lightly spritz the bottom of a 7-inch form pan.

3. Pick the first tortilla shell and place it on the pan's bottom. Add celery, shredded chicken and a scoop of blue cheese dressing. Repeat layering and you can add some more wing sauce to the layer as you move on. Add sharp cheddar cheese on top.

4. Pour a cup of water into the pot. Place the pan on a trivet, then lower the pan into the pot and switch to high pressure for about 15 minutes. Quick release the pressure and allow to sit for five minutes prior to serving. If desired, add lettuce or more celery, blue cheese and carrots on top.

3. INSTANT POT CHICKEN SPINACH PARMESAN ORZO

Preparation Time: 15 minutes | Cooking Time: 17 minutes | Serves: 6

Ingredients

- 12 ounces orzo pasta, uncooked
- 3 cups spinach, chopped
- 1 tablespoon olive oil
- 1 ½ pounds chicken breasts
- 1 cup Parmesan cheese, shredded
- 1 tablespoon minced garlic
- ½ cup chicken broth
- 1 tsp kosher salt
- 1 cup diced onion
- 1 tsp Italian seasoning
- 14.5 oz. (1) can petite diced tomatoes, best with fire roasted
- ½ tsp black pepper
- 2 ¾ cups water

Instructions

1. Switch the pot to sauté setting. Once the displays indicates hot, pour in olive oil and then swirl pot around. Place in onion and let to sauté for four minutes. Place in garlic and then sauté for 20 seconds. Use chicken broth to deglaze the pot.

2. Spread a layer of chicken on the pot's bottom. Drizzle Italian seasoning, pepper and salt over chicken. Add tomatoes atop the chicken.

3. Into a pan that can fit into the instant pot, add water and orzo. Then lower pan atop the chicken as evenly as you can using a sling. You can cover the pan.

4. Use a lid to cover the pot and seal. Be sure valve is set to sealing. Switch the pressure/manual cook to 15 minutes for frozen chicken and 12 minutes for thawed chicken. When time is over, leave the pot to stand for five minutes before pushing the valve to venting position. Take out the lid.

5. Take out the orzo pan with hot pads and reserve.

6. Slice chicken into pieces. Mix spinach and parmesan into pot. Then mix orzo into the pot. Season with pepper and salt.

7. Transfer onto serving plates.

4. INSTANT POT SWEET AND SOUR PINEAPPLE CHICKEN

Preparation Time: 15 minutes | Cooking Time: 15 minutes | Serves: 4

Ingredients

- 4 chopped green onions
- 1 cup fresh diced pineapple, you can also use canned
- 2 chicken breasts medium sized and chopped into one inch pieces
- 1 tablespoon olive oil
- 2 cloves minced garlic
- 3 tablespoon rice vinegar
- 1 cup jasmine rice, dry
- 2 tablespoon ketchup
- 3 tablespoon brown sugar
- 1 each yellow, green and red bell pepper, sliced
- 2 tablespoon low sodium soy sauce
- 1 ¼ cups chicken broth

Instructions

1. Into the instant pot, add the following in this order, olive oil, chicken, pineapple, rice vinegar, brown sugar, ketchup, garlic, soy sauce, broth and rice. The rice should be floating on top. Cover with a lid and let the contents to cook on high pressure for two minutes.

2. The pot will come to pressure for around ten minutes and then cook for 2 minutes on high pressure. Once done, quick release the pressure and take out the lid carefully to avoid burn. Rice may seem crunchy or uncooked at this point. Ensure you mix in the bells peppers, cover with lid and allow to stand for about 5 to 10 minutes to absorb the extra liquid. The rice will eventually cook at the end.

3. Uncover and distribute into 4 bowls. Add green onions on top and serve.

5. INSTANT POT CHICKEN BREASTS PLUS GRAVY

Preparation Time: 5 minutes | Cooking Time: 10 minutes | Serves: 3

Ingredients

- 3 chicken breasts, boneless skinless
- 2 tablespoons avocado or canola divided
- 1 cup water or lager or light beer pilsner
- ½ teaspoon oregano
- ½ teaspoon garlic powder
- 1/2 teaspoon paprika
- ½ teaspoon black pepper
- 1/2 teaspoon cumin
- 1 teaspoon salt

Gravy

- 1 tablespoon cornstarch
- Pepper and salt to taste
- 1 tablespoon water

Instructions

1. Mix the spices and salt with one tablespoon of oil to form a paste. Brush the chicken breasts with the paste.

2. Switch the pot to sauté setting and then heat oil. When the oil is hot, place in the chicken breasts.

3. Brown chicken on each side for about two to three minutes per side and then take it out from the pot.

4. Pour the beer into the pot and scrape up the browned bits from the pot's bottom.

5. Put the trivet inside the pot and place back the chicken into the pot onto the trivet. Press the cancel button.

6. Cover with lid and seal. Move the vent to the sealing position. Then push the manual button for high pressure and set time to five minutes (ten minutes if using shredded chicken). The pot will take around ten minutes to reach full pressure before a countdown timer is displayed.

7. After five minutes elapse, natural release the pressure for eight minutes ten minutes for larger chicken breasts). Release the remaining pressure.

8. Take out the chicken from pot and let to sit for around five minutes prior to serving. This will allow the juices to redistribute.

Gravy:

1. Mix the cornstarch and water until the resulting mixture is smooth.

2. Switch the pot to the sauté setting and then heat the cooking liquids to simmer. Pour in the cornstarch-water mixture. Let to cook for around 3 to 5 minutes. Add pepper and salt to taste.

For shredded chicken

Omit the gravy step. Place the chicken in a large bowl containing half cup of cooking liquid and then use two forks to shred. Alternatively, you can shred chicken with the paddle attachment of the mixer.

Tip: Five minutes of cooking works well with average sized six ounce chicken breasts. Increase the cooking time by one to two minutes for larger breasts.

6. INSTANT POT CREAMY SALSA CHICKEN

Preparation Time: 10 minutes | Cooking Time: 20 to 28 minutes | Serves: 1

Ingredients

- ½ cup sour cream
- 2 tablespoon cornstarch
- 2 pounds boneless, skinless chicken breasts
- ¼ cup lime juice
- ½ cup broth or water
- 1 cup picante sauce
- chopped cilantro and grated cheddar, if desired

Instructions

1. Pour water into an instant pot and then add the chicken. Spread picante sauce atop the chicken.

2. Cover the pot with a lid and ensure the valve is at the sealing position. Switch the manual/pressure cook to 18 minutes for frozen chicken and 15 minutes for thawed chicken. Once the time has elapsed, allow the pot to stand for about 5 to 10 minutes before moving valve to the venting position.

3. Take out the lid and then shred chicken. Mix in lime juice and sour cream. In case you prefer a thicker sauce, set to sauté setting and pour in a mixture of 2 tablespoon cold water and 2 tablespoon of cornstarch without any lumps. Mix until thickened.

4. You can serve the chicken and sauce together with rice atop tortillas with cilantro and cheddar if desired.

Tip: Feel free to use boneless thighs or bone-in chicken. Just like breast it can be thawed or frozen.

7. INSTANT POT CHICKEN TERIYAKI RECIPE

Preparation Time: 5 minutes | Cooking Time: 6 minutes | Serves: 4

Ingredients

- 1 1/2 lbs. boneless and skinless chicken thighs
- 1 1/2 tablespoon cooking oil
- 1 1/2 tablespoons sugar
- 2 1/2 tablespoons soy sauce
- 1/2 cup mirin
- white sesame seeds, for garnishing if desired
- 1 teaspoon corn starch and 1 tablespoon water combine thoroughly

Instructions

1. Set the instant pot to the sauté setting. Pour in cooking oil once the pot is heated fully (will prevent chicken from sticking on the pot). Then pan sear chicken thighs until they have turned brown on the outside. In case the chicken sticks too much onto the pot, pan sear with a non-stick skillet or omit this step.

2. Add sugar, mirin, and soy sauce. Cover with lid, choose manual and set to 6 minutes on high pressure.

3. Once the pot beeps, set to quick release. Uncover carefully after the valve drops. Change the pot to sauté setting. Pour in corn starch slurry and mix to thicken the sauce. Switch the heat off. If using, stud chicken with sesame seeds and then serve right away along with steamed rice.

8. INSTANT POT CREAMY GARLIC CHICKEN THIGHS

Preparation Time: 10 minutes | Cooking Time: 5 minutes | Serves: 4

Ingredients

- ground black pepper
- 1 1/2 lbs. chicken thighs, skinless, boneless and fat trimmed off
- 1/2 cup chicken broth
- salt
- 1/3 cup heavy whipping cream
- 2 tablespoons olive oil
- 1/4 teaspoon salt or more to suit your taste
- 12 cloves peeled garlic
- 3 tablespoons Kraft grated Parmesan cheese
- 1/2 tablespoon paprika, smoked
- 2 sprigs rosemary

Instructions

1. Remove excess fat from chicken thighs with kitchen scissors. Season with pepper and salt on each side of the thighs.

2. Set the instant pot to sauté setting. Then add olive oil after the pot is heated fully (this will prevent the meat from sticking onto the pot). Pan sear the chicken thighs until they are browned a bit. (You can also use a non-stick or regular skillet to pan fry the chicken).

3. Add chicken broth, rosemary and garlic into the pot. Drizzle paprika over the chicken. Cover pot and set manual to high pressure for five minutes.

4. Do a quick release after the pot beeps. Once the valve has dropped, uncover carefully and then add grated parmesan cheese, salt and heavy whipping cream. Mix the contents thoroughly. Set to sauté mode for several minutes to thicken the sauce. Season to taste with salt and then serve right away.

9. HONEY SESAME INSTANT POT CHICKEN

Preparation Time: 5 minutes | Cooking Time: 8 minutes | Serves: 1

Ingredients

- 1 tablespoon chopped scallion
- 1 1/2 lbs. chicken thighs, without skin and bones
- 1 teaspoon toasted white sesame
- salt
- 1 1/2 tablespoon oil
- ground black pepper
- 2 cloves garlic, minced

Honey Sesame Sauce

- 1 teaspoon corn starch
- 1/2 cup chicken broth
- 1 tablespoon apple cider vinegar
- 2 tablespoons soy sauce
- 2 1/2 tablespoons honey
- 1/2 teaspoon dark soy sauce
- 1 teaspoon sesame oil
- 1 teaspoon chili garlic sauce or Sriracha, Rooster brand, or more to suit your taste

Instructions

1. Wash chicken thighs and then rinse with cool water. Then pat dry on paper towels. Add pepper and salt to the chicken and reserve. Combine together all ingredients in the sauce. Mix thoroughly. Be sure that the cornstarch and honey are dissolved completely. Reserve.

2. Set the instant pot to the sauté setting. Add cooking oil to the pot once heated fully (this will prevent the chicken from sticking onto the pot). Pan fry the chicken until browned a bit. (You can pan fry on a non-stick skillet or omit this step if the meat sticks too much on the pot). Place in garlic and then sauté for a while. Add the sauce and then add white sesame. Cover and set the manual to high pressure for eight minutes.

3. Quick release once the pot beeps. Then carefully uncover after the valve has dropped. Pour chopped scallion into the pot and then serve right away. Switch pot to the sauté setting for 2 minutes to thicken the sauce a bit.

4. In case the sauce seems lighter, you can add a little dark soy sauce to make it darker. The color of soy sauce varies whereby some are darker while others are lighter.

10. INSTANT POT GINGER SOY CHICKEN

Preparation Time: 10 minutes | Cooking Time: 8 minutes | Serves: 3

Ingredients

- 2 tablespoons soy sauce
- 1 1/2 lbs. chicken wings and drumsticks (alternatively, use chicken thighs or chicken breast)
- 1/2 cup water
- 1 teaspoon sesame oil
- 1 inch piece ginger, peeled and chopped into slices
- 1 tablespoon oil
- 1 stalk scallion, chopped into two-inch lengths
- 3 tablespoon Indonesian kecap manis or sweet soy sauce
- 3 dashes ground white pepper

Instructions

1. Start by cutting the drumsticks into 2 to 3 slices.

2. Set the instant pot to the sauté setting. Add cooking oil immediately the pot is heated fully. Sear chicken in pan until browned a bit. Place in ginger and then sauté for a few minutes. Add sesame oil, sweet soy sauce, soy sauce, ground white pepper and water. Cover your pot and set manual to high pressure for eight minutes.

3. Quick release after the pot beeps. Carefully uncover once the valve has dropped. In case the sauce is too thin, change to sauté mode for about 1 minute to reduce sauce.

11. INSTANT POT CREAMY SUN DRIED TOMATOES CHICKEN

Preparation Time: 10 minutes | Cooking Time: 10 minutes | Serves: 4

Ingredients

- 2 tablespoons grated Parmesan cheese
- 1 1/2 - 2 lbs. chicken thighs
- 1/2 cup chicken broth
- ground black pepper
- salt
- 1/2 cup heavy whipping cream
- 1 tablespoon olive oil
- 3 sprigs thyme
- 1/4 teaspoon salt or to taste
- 3 cloves minced garlic
- 1/2 cup sun dried tomatoes along with its oil

Instructions

1. Season each side of thicken with pepper and salt.

2. Set the instant pot to sauté mode. Then add ½ tablespoon of olive oil immediately the pot is heated fully. Pan sear the thighs first with the skin down, until each side is browned. (Alternatively, you can pan fry the chicken on non-stick skillet or regular skillet over stove top). Spoon out the excess grease from the pot and discard.

3. Pour in remaining olive oil, add garlic and sauté for a while. Add sun dried tomatoes, salt, thyme, heavy whipping cream and chicken broth. Cover, choose manual and set to high pressure for ten minutes.

4. Quick release once the pot beeps. Uncover carefully after the valve has dropped. Switch to sauté setting, pour in grated parmesan cheese and let to cook for two minutes. You can serve right away.

12. SUPER EASY INSTANT POT SHRIMP SCAMPI FOOD DINNER RECIPES

Preparation Time: 10 minutes | Cooking Time: 1-3 minutes | Serves: 1

Ingredients

- 2 tablespoons butter
- 1lb de-veined and peeled shrimp with tail on
- 3 garlic cloves minced
- 1/2 Lemmon
- 1/4 cup dry white wine
- kosher salt
- fresh ground pepper
- 1/2 cup chicken broth
- dried parsley

Instructions

1. Set the pot to sauté mode. Add butter when pot is hot and melt. Add garlic and sauté until brown.

2. Pour in wine and the sauté until the smell of alcohol fades away. You can use any white wine you prefer. Once the alcohol boils away, it will leave a sweet taste and flavor.

3. Add shrimp along with chicken broth. Then add two pinches kosher salt and pepper to taste.

4. Cover with lid and seal. Let to cook for 1 minute on high pressure. Cook for 3 minutes if frozen.

5. Then quick release the pressure and sauté once again until the sauce begins to simmer.

6. Add parsley and half Lemmon juice. You can add as much parsley as you desire. Combine together and serve.

13. SALMON AND VEGETABLES WITH LEMON-BUTTER SAUCE

Preparation Time: 10 minutes | Cooking Time: 5 minutes | Serves: 5

Ingredients

- 5 salmon fillets, frozen and 4 ounce each
- 1 cup low sodium vegetable broth
- 2 lemons juiced
- 2 lbs. medium red potatoes, chopped into one inch chunks
- 1 teaspoon fine sea salt
- 4 tablespoon melted unsalted butter
- 4 carrot pieces, peeled and cut into 1 inch thick (around two cups)
- freshly ground black pepper
- Fresh chopped dill for garnish (if desired)
- 1/2 teaspoon garlic powder

Instructions

1. Add broth inside the inner pot and then add carrots and potatoes. Add salmon fillets atop the veggies with the skin-side down.

2. Spread melted butter on top of salmon. Drizzle garlic powder and salt on top.

3. Cover with lid. Then select Manual or pressure cook. Adjust high pressure and set time to five minutes. Be sure that steam release valve is in the sealing position. When cooking is done, release the pressure naturally for ten minutes before doing a quick release to remove the remaining pressure.

4. Uncover the pot. Serve right away studded with dill and black pepper or put the salmon and veggies in an airtight container and then chill for maximum of four days.

Note: In case the salmon fillets are more than four ounces, you may be able to fit only 4 inside the pot at one time. In addition, ensure you chop the veggies and potatoes into small pieces so that they can cook during the short cooking time.

14. SCALLOPS WITH HERB TOMATO SAUCE

Preparation Time: 10 minutes | Cooking Time: 13 minutes | Serves: 4

Ingredients

- 1 1/2 lbs. fresh scallops, cleaned and drained
- 3 1/2 cups peeled fresh tomatoes
- 1 medium peeled and diced red onion
- 1 clove garlic minced
- 6 ounces tomato paste, 1 can
- 1/4 cup dry red wine
- 1 tablespoon fresh oregano, chopped
- 2 tablespoon fresh Italian parsley, chopped
- 2 tablespoons vegetable oil
- Hot cooked rice or pasta (if desired)
- 1 teaspoon salt
- 1/4 teaspoon black pepper

Instructions

1. Push the sauté button and then heat the oil in the Instant Pot. Add garlic and onion and then cook while stirring for about 3 to 4 minutes or until the onion is translucent and soft. Add oregano, tomatoes, parsley, wine, tomato paste, pepper and salt. Combine thoroughly.

2. Close the lid and push the pressure release valve to the sealing position. Set to high pressure and cook for 8 minutes.

3. After cooking is done, push the Cancel button and do a quick release. Check the taste of the sauce and you can add more pepper and salt as desired.

4. Push the sauté button and then place the scallops into the pot. Cook for one minute or until the sauce starts to simmer. Push the Cancel button. Cover the pot with its lid and leave to sit for about 8 minutes or until the scallops become opaque. If desired, serve on top of pasta.

15. INSTANT POT SALMON WITH GARLIC POTATOES AND GREENS

Preparation Time: 10 minutes | Cooking Time: 5-7 minutes | Serves: 4

Ingredients

- 4 5- to 6-ounce skin-on center-chopped salmon fillets (about 3/4 to 1 inch thick)
- 1 1/4 pounds small red-skinned potatoes, chopped in half or quarters
- 1/2 teaspoon grated lemon zest and wedges, for serving
- freshly ground pepper and Kosher salt
- 4 cloves minced garlic
- 1/4 teaspoon paprika
- 4 tablespoons butter, unsalted
- 4 cups packed mixed baby spinach and arugula (around 3 1/2 ounces)

Instructions

1. Place potatoes into your Instant Pot. Add 1/2 teaspoon salt, 2 tablespoons butter, several grinds of pepper and 1 cup of water. Put the steam rack of the pot on top of potatoes.

2. Brush the sides and top of salmon fillets with lemon zest and paprika. Generously season with pepper and salt. Transfer onto the rack with the skin-side down. Close the lid and ensure the steam valve moved to the seal position. Set the pot to high pressure for three minutes. Once done, gently switch steam valve to vent position to release the pressure.

3. Take out the salmon and the rack. Then set pot to sauté mode at normal heat. Once the potatoes begin to sizzle, add garlic and let to cook while stirring for 1 to 2 minutes until softened. Mix in the remaining two tablespoons of butter and then generously season with pepper and salt. Use a wooden spoon or fork to smash the potatoes until they are chunky.

4. Switch the cooker off. Transfer the mixed greens to potatoes and mix for 1 to 2 minutes until wilted. Add pepper and salt to taste. Distribute salmon and potato mixture into plates and then serve along with lemon wedges.

16. INSTANT POT SHRIMP BOIL

Preparation Time: 15 minutes | Cooking Time: 20 minutes | Serves: 4-6

Ingredients

- 1 1/2 pounds medium shrimp with shell
- 2 tablespoons fresh parsley leaves, chopped
- 1 tablespoon hot sauce
- 1 (12.8-ounce) package smoked andouille sausage, chopped thinly
- 1/2 medium sweet onion, chopped
- 4 teaspoons Old Bay seasoning, divided
- 1/4 cup butter, unsalted
- 1 lemon, cut into wedges
- 1 (16-ounce) lager or pilsner
- 1 1/2 pounds baby red potatoes
- 3 cloves garlic, minced
- 3 ears corn, halved

Instructions

1. Into an Instant Pot, add 3 teaspoons Old Bay seasoning, potatoes, hot sauce, sausage, and onion. Toss until mixed well. Add corn and beer on top.

2. Select the setting for manual and set to high pressure for five minutes. After cooking is done, do a quick-release as directed by the pot's manufacturer.

3. Add the shrimp. Set pot to high pressure for one minute. Once cooking is done, do a quick-release as directed by the manufacturer.

4. Over medium low heat, melt the butter in a small skillet. Then mix in the remaining 1 teaspoon of Old Bay seasoning and garlic for around 1 to 2 minutes until fragrant.

5. Serve the shrimp mixture right away, sprinkled with the butter mixture, studded with lemon and parsley if desired.

17. INSTANT POT SHRIMP RISOTTO

Preparation Time: 10 minutes | Cooking Time: 16.5 minutes | Serves: 1

Ingredients

- 1 1/2 cups arborio rice
- 1 pound large shrimp, peeled and deveined
- 1 shallot
- 4 tablespoons butter, unsalted
- 2 cloves garlic
- freshly ground pepper and Kosher salt
- 1 8-ounce bottle clam juice
- 1/2 teaspoon finely grated lemon zest and some more for topping
- 3 sprigs thyme, fresh
- 1/2 cup peas, frozen
- Lemon wedges, for serving
- 1/3 cup dry white wine
- 2 tablespoons grated parmesan cheese

Instructions

1. Switch the pot to sauté on the medium setting. Cut garlic and shallot. Once the pot become hot, add two tablespoons of butter, followed by the shallot, garlic and a dash each of pepper and salt. Cook while stirring for about 3 minutes until softened. Mix in the thyme sprigs and rice and let to cook for about 3 minutes until rice becomes toasted. Mix in wine and scrape the pot's bottom. Cook for about 30 seconds until evaporated. Switch the sauté function off.

2. Mix three cups of hot water and clam juice into the pot. Cover with lid and move steam valve to the seal position. Set pot to cook for 5 minutes on high pressure. When cooking is done, move the valve to the vent position to completely release steam. Gently open the lid.

3. Season shrimp with pepper and salt and then transfer into the pot. Mix in peas. With the Instant Pot still switched off, cover with lid and leave shrimp to cook through for approximately five minutes.

4. Add lemon zest and parmesan into the risotto. Mix in remaining two tablespoons of butter until it has melted. If need be, add some dashes of water to loosen up. Get rid of thyme sprigs. Distribute into bowls. Add lemon zest on top and then serve along with lemon wedges.

BEEF AND PORK

1. THE EASIEST INSTANT POT MEATBALLS

Preparation Time: 15 minutes | Cooking Time: 5 minutes | Serves: 1

Ingredients

- 1 ½ cups barbecue sauce
- 2 teaspoons garlic powder
- 2 pounds ground beef
- ½ teaspoon ground black pepper
- 1 teaspoon fine sea salt

Instructions

1. Start by folding ground beef into one inch balls. Then put them in a single layer in the pressure cooker. The balls can touch each other.

2. Drizzle onto the meatballs with black pepper, sea salt, and garlic powder. Top with barbecue sauce. Cover the cooker with a lid and ensure the pressure knob is at the seal position. Switch the pressure/cook function to high pressure and set the time to five minutes.

3. Once 5 minutes elapses, the cooker will beep. Switch the pressure knob from sealing to vent position to quick release the pressure. Take care not to be burned by steam.

4. You can serve together with a leafy green salad of your choice.

2. INSTANT POT SMOKED SAUSAGE COUNTRY BOIL

Preparation Time: 15 minutes | Cooking Time: 1 minute | Serves: 4 to 6

Ingredients

- 1 (13 oz.) package smoked sausage, chopped into ½ inch rounds
- 1 ½ pounds petite red potatoes, cleaned and chopped in half
- ½ pound fresh green beans, cleaned and then trimmed
- 1 teaspoon seasoned salt
- 1 bay leaf
- 3 ears of corn, husked and then chopped into thirds
- ½ teaspoon celery seed
- 2 tablespoons butter, chopped into 8 small pieces
- 1 teaspoon smoked paprika
- ½ teaspoon black pepper
- 1 teaspoon dried parsley
- ½ teaspoon onion powder
- 1 cup broth or water
- 1 teaspoon garlic powder

Instructions

1. Mix smoked paprika, onion powder, garlic powder, parsley, celery seed, salt and pepper together in a small bowl.

2. Add water to the bottom of the pot and place in the bay leaf.

3. Pour in potatoes in an even layer. Drizzle about ½ the seasonings onto potatoes. Place in sausage in an even layer. Pour in green beans evenly on top. Drizzle the remaining seasonings over the beans. Place in corn evenly on top. Drizzle the remaining seasonings over corn. Top with butter.

4. Cover with a lid and ensure valve is moved to the sealing position. Switch manual/pressure to one minute. Instant pot will come to pressure in a short while. When the one minute cook time is done, push valve to the venting position. Take out the lid.

5. Use tongs to toss the contents inside the pot. Spoon onto the serving dishes. Top each serving with a tablespoon of drippings.

3. INSTANT POT MEATBALLS AND RED POTATOES WITH CREAMY PARMESAN SAUCE

Preparation Time: 20 minutes | Cooking Time: 3 minutes | Serves: 6 to 8

Ingredients

- 1 pound frozen cooked meatballs (You can use Costco meatballs)
- 1 cup grated or shredded Parmesan cheese
- 2 tablespoon butter
- 1 pound red potatoes
- 8 to 12 ounces chopped white mushrooms
- ¼ cup cornstarch
- 1 cup half and half
- ½ pound green beans, fresh
- 1 ½ cups chicken broth
- 2 teaspoon garlic powder
- Pepper and salt

Instructions

1. Switch the pot to sauté setting and when the display indicates hot, place in butter. Swirl around until the butter has melted. Pour in mushrooms, then drizzle garlic powder on top and sauté for about 3 to 5 minutes.

2. As the mushrooms cook, prepare the red potatoes. Start by cleaning them and then chop into about 1 ½ inch pieces or into quarters. Wash the green beans and then trim them.

3. Pour the broth, beans, potatoes and meatballs into the instant pot. Stir.

4. Cover pot with a lid and be sure it's secure. Ensure the valve is moved to the sealing position. Adjust the manual/pressure to high pressure for three minutes. Pot will come to pressure in around ten minutes. Once done, do a quick release and then uncover the pot. Change the pot to sauté.

5. In the microwave or on the stove, heat half and half until warm. You can microwave for a minute. Then mix cornstarch with half and half until the resulting mix is smooth. Mix parmesan cheese and half and half mixture into the instant pot. Sauce will become thick almost right away. Switch off the sauté setting when it becomes thick.

6. Season with pepper and salt.

7. Spoon into serving dishes and serve.

4. HAWAIIAN KALUA PORK RECIPE

Preparation Time: 10 minutes | Cooking Time: 60 minutes | Serves: 4

Ingredients

- 2 lbs. pork roast
- 1/2 tablespoon kosher salt
- 2 tablespoons soy sauce
- 1 tablespoon oil
- 1/2 cup water
- 2 tablespoons Wright's Hickory Liquid Smoke
- 2 tablespoons brown sugar

Instructions

1. Choose browning and then pour oil into the instant pot. Once the oil becomes hot, add pork and brown on each side for approximately 3 minutes per side. Transfer onto a platter after browning.

2. Switch off the cooker and add liquid smoke, brown sugar, soy sauce, and water. Place in the browned pork along with its juice. Drizzle salt over the pork.

3. Set to high pressure for 1 hour. Once the pot beeps, natural release the pressure inside for around 20 minutes. Carefully take out the lid when valve drops.

4. Remove meat from the pot and then use two forks to shred it. Serve right away along with steamed rice.

5. INSTANT POT SPICE-RUBBED PORK CHOPS WITH VEGGIES

Preparation Time: 8 minutes | Cooking Time: 20 minutes | Serves: 6

Ingredients

For the vegetables

- 1.5 lb. potato trio (blue, yellow and red creamer potatoes), cut in half
- 1½ tablespoon rapeseed oil, divided
- 1 tablespoon dried thyme
- 2 medium zucchinis, cut at around half inch and then halved
- 2 teaspoons smoked paprika
- 1 tablespoon dried parsley
- 1½ teaspoons ground black pepper
- 1 tablespoon dried rosemary
- 2 teaspoons Himalayan Sea Salt
- 1 tablespoon dried basil
- 1 lb. baby carrots, halved lengthwise
- 1 tablespoon dried oregano

For the pork chops

- 6 open nature boneless pork chops (1.5 lb.)
- 1 tablespoon butter
- 1 tablespoon grapeseed oil
- 1½ teaspoons dried basil
- 2 teaspoons garlic salt
- 2 tablespoons garlic, minced
- 1½ teaspoons lemon pepper
- ¼ cup low sodium chicken broth
- 1 teaspoon brown sugar
- 1½ teaspoons smoked paprika

Instructions

1. Set the instant pot to the sauté function.

2. Pour in one tablespoon grapeseed oil and then heat it up. Add halved potatoes and then sauté lightly while stirring often to prevent them from sticking.

3. When 2 to 3 minutes elapse, pour in halved carrots. Sauté the carrots and potatoes for around two minutes.

4. As they are sautéing, in a medium bowl, add half tablespoon of grapeseed oil along with all the seasonings for the vegetables.

5. Switch off the Instant Pot and then transfer to the bowl containing the seasonings. Toss together while adding the chopped zucchini until mixed well. Reserve.

6. Turn the pot on again and set to the sauté function. Add the grapeseed oil and the butter.

7. Season each side of pork chops with the brown sugar, garlic salt, dried basil, lemon pepper, and smoked paprika.

8. Transfer to the pot and then brown each side of pork chops for around 2 to 3 minutes per side.

9. When second side is browned, add minced garlic on top and spread chicken broth all over the top.

10. Use aluminum foil to loosely wrap the oiled and seasoned vegetables. Put the pot's basket over the chops and place the wrapped vegetables on top of the basket.

11. Turn on the instant pot and then set to high pressure for six minutes. Cover pot with lid and ensure you have closed the steam release button.

12. When time is up, quick release to allow escape of steam and then uncover the pot.

13. Gently take out the foil packets and then open them into a serving dish. Take out the wire basket, gently remove chops and place them into a serving dish.

14. If desired, you can make a gravy using the remaining juice. You just need to prepare a slurry with water and cornstarch and then mix it into remaining juice until it becomes a bit thinner than the consistency you desire. Add the gravy on top of the pork chops.

15. Serve.

6. INSTANT POT HK GARLIC BEEF RICE BOWL (POT IN POT)

Preparation Time: 10 minutes | Cooking Time: 70 minutes | Serves: 2-4

Ingredients

- 200 grams frozen mixed veggies
- 1¼ pound chuck roast steak, with thickness of 1.5 inch
- 1 small diced onion
- 1 whole minced garlic, around 12 cloves
- 1 (15 ml) tablespoon peanut oil
- ground black pepper and Kosher salt to taste
- 2 tablespoons unsalted butter

Chicken stock mixture

- 1 tablespoon (15ml) light soy sauce, not low sodium soy sauce
- 1 teaspoon (5ml) Worcestershire sauce
- ¾ cup (188ml) unsalted chicken stock

Thickener

- 2 tablespoons (30ml) cold water
- 2 tablespoons (18g) cornstarch

Pot in Pot Rice

- 1 cup (250 ml) cold running tap water
- 230 grams (about 1 cup) Jasmine rice

Instructions

1. Heat the instant pot on medium high heat (Hit sauté button and then switch to sauté more function). Wait until the pot displays hot. .

2. Prepare the ingredients while the pot heats. You should take about 24 minutes and this includes time for browning chuck steak.

3. Generously season one side of chuck steak with freshly ground black pepper and kosher salt. Pour one tablespoon of peanut oil into the pot. Make sure you coat the whole bottom of the pot with the oil. Gently transfer seasoned side of chuck steak into the pot. Season generously the remaining side with freshly ground black pepper and kosher salt. Let to brown for six mins per side without turning. Take out and reserve in a large mixing bowl.

4. Preparing the chicken stock mixture: As the chuck steak is browns in pot, combine one tablespoon of light soy sauce and one teaspoon of Worcestershire sauce with ¾ cup of unsalted chicken stock.

5. Adjust the heat to medium. (Push the cancel button, press sauté button and then set to the Sauté Normal Setting). Pour the diced onion into the pot and then sauté for one minute. Place in 2 tablespoon of unsalted butter and melt it. Pour in minced garlic cloves and then stir for about 90 seconds until fragrant. Avoid burning the garlic. If desired, season with freshly ground black pepper and kosher salt.

6. Add in half cup of chicken stock mixture and then deglaze completely the pot's bottom by scrubbing the brown bits using a wooden spoon. Add in remaining ¼ cup of chicken stock mixture.

7. After you deglaze, chop chuck steak into about 1.5 to 2 inches cubes. Transfer all the chuck stew meat along with meat juice to the instant pot.

8. Place a stainless steel bowl that is filled with one cup Jasmine rice atop a steamer rack. Pour one cup of cold water into the rice bowl. Ensure water covers all rice. Cover with lid and then cook for 32 minutes at High Pressure. Natural release for 10 minutes. Switch the heat off and then release any remaining pressure. Gently open the lid, fluff and reserve the cooked rice.

9. Place the frozen mixed veggies into the Instant Pot to warm up for about 30 seconds. Push the cancel button and then set to sauté mode to heat the sauce. Combine cornstarch with water in a small mixing bowl and then stir the mix into HK Garlic Sauce, one third at a time until the thickness desired is achieved. Check the taste and adjust with kosher salt if need be.

10. Put the beef and mixed veggies on top of Jasmine rice and sprinkle with the HK Garlic Sauce. Serve right away.

7. INSTANT POT SPARE RIBS AND RICE

Preparation Time: 5 minutes | Cooking Time: 35 minutes | Serves: 4-6

Ingredients

- 1½ cup rinsed Jasmine rice
- 1 pound pork spare ribs , chopped into pieces
- 1½ cup cold water
- 1 tablespoon oil

Black Bean Marinade

- 3 minced garlic cloves
- 1.5 tablespoon black bean sauce
- 1 teaspoon sugar
- 1 tablespoon water or Shaoxing wine
- 1 tablespoon regular soy sauce
- 1 tablespoon grated ginger

- A pinch white pepper
- 1 teaspoon fish sauce (if using)
- 1 teaspoon sesame oil

Garnish

- 1 Thai chili, finely sliced (If using)
- Finely chopped green onions

Instructions

1. Marinate the spare ribs with the Black Bean Marinade in a mixing bowl for a minimum of half an hour and up to overnight in your refrigerator.

2. Combine the marinated ribs together with one tablespoon of oil and transfer into the Instant Pot. You can place a single layer of spare ribs to fill the whole bottom of the Instant Pot. Then spread a layer of 1½ cup Jasmine rice over spare ribs. Pour in 1½ cup of cold water. In case rice is rinsed and drained well, add 1 1/4 cup of cold water instead. Make sure all rice is covered with liquid. Cook for 13 minutes at High Pressure and then natural release for 10 minutes.

Tip: Be sure the spare ribs are on the bottom and rice on top.

3. Fluff and then gently combine the rice and spare ribs. Check the taste and add more soy sauce or salt if need be. Stud with finely chopped green onion and spice it up with Thai chili. Serve right away.

8. INSTANT POT SWEET 'N SOUR PORK CHOPS

Preparation Time: 20 minutes | Cooking Time: 32 minutes | Serves: 4

Ingredients

- 1 teaspoon Worcestershire sauce
- 4 pounded pork chops , boneless or bone-in
- 1 chopped green/red bell pepper
- 1 tablespoon tomato paste
- 1 small onion, sliced
- 3 minced garlic cloves
- 1.5 tablespoon white sugar
- ¾ cup cold water
- 1 tablespoon olive oil or peanut oil
- ¼ cup ketchup
- ⅔ cup canned pineapple chunks
- 1 tablespoon Chinese light soy sauce or regular soy sauce
- ¼ cup white vinegar

Marinade:

- ¼ teaspoon sesame oil
- ¼ teaspoon kosher salt

- 1 tablespoon Chinese light soy sauce or regular soy sauce
- ½ teaspoon white sugar

Thickener:

- 3 tablespoons cold water
- 2.5 tablespoons cornstarch

Instructions

1. Pound each side of pork chops with force using a meat tenderizer or backend of a heavy knife.

2. Marinate the pork chops with 1 tablespoon soy sauce, ½ teaspoon white sugar, ¼ teaspoon of sesame oil, and ¼ teaspoon of salt for a minimum of half an hour. Place in a refrigerator if marinating for about 1 1/2 to 8 hours.

3. Over medium heat, heat the instant pot (set to the sauté normal function). Be sure the pot displays a hot sign. This will keep the pork chops from sticking to pot.

4. Add 1 tablespoon of peanut oil and make sure the oil coats the entire bottom of pot. Brown two marinated pork chops for about 75 to 90 seconds on each side (avoid flipping them constantly). Take out and reserve. Repeat this with the rest of the pork chops.

5. Add a pinch of kosher salt, chopped onions and ground black pepper if using. Let the onions cook for about one minute until softened. Place in the minced garlic cloves and then sauté for about 30 seconds until fragrant.

6. Pour in ⅔ cup of cold water and then deglaze by scrubbing off all the brown bits from the bottom.

7. Add 1 tablespoon of tomato paste, ¼ cup of ketchup, 1 teaspoon of Worcestershire sauce, ¼ cup of white vinegar, 1 tablespoons of soy sauce, and 1.5 tablespoons of white sugar. Combine everything well. Add the pork chops along with the meat juice into the pot. Cook for 1 minute at high Pressure and then natural release for 10 minutes.

8. Take out the pork chops. Hit cancel and press sauté to heat up the sauce. Add chopped green/red pepper and ⅔ cup of pineapple chunks. Mix and let to cook for 1 minute.

9. To thicken the sauce, combine 3 tablespoons of cold water with 2.5 tablespoons of cornstarch. Combine it in one third at a time until you get the thickness desired. Check the taste for the sweet 'n sour sauce and add more vinegar, sugar or salt as desired. You should use two pinches of kosher salt. Switch the heat off. Place back the pork chops and then coat with the sauce.

10. To serve, sprinkle sweet 'n sour sauce atop pork chops and serve.

9. INSTANT POT BARBACOA BEEF

Preparation Time: 20 minutes | Cooking Time: 1 hour 25 minutes | Serves: 2-4

Ingredients

- 3 pounds fat trimmed beef chuck roast, chopped into 2-inch chunks
- 2 tablespoons apple cider vinegar
- 2/3 cup water or beer
- 2 chipotles in adobo sauce or more to suit your taste
- 4 cloves garlic
- 1 small white onion, peeled and chopped roughly
- 1 tablespoon regular oregano or dried Mexican oregano
- 1/4 teaspoon ground cloves
- 1 tablespoon olive oil
- 1 teaspoon black pepper
- 4-ounce (1 can) sliced green chiles

- 3 bay leaves
- 1 tablespoon ground cumin
- 1/4 cup fresh lime juice
- 2 teaspoons salt

Instructions

1. in a food processor or blender, mix cloves, oregano, cumin, beer, vinegar, garlic, lime juice, chipotles, pepper, salt, onion, and green chiles. Then purée for about 30 seconds or until smooth completely. Reserve.

2. Hit the sauté function on the instant pot and then add oil. When the oil shimmers, add roast and then sear while flipping after every 45 to 60 seconds until roast turns brown on all sides. Hit cancel switch the heat off.

3. Place in the pureed sauce and bay leaves. Toss everything briefly until roast is coated evenly in the sauce. Cover with lid and push to the sealing position.

4. Set the pot to high pressure for 60 minutes. Let to cook. Gently move the vent to the venting position to quick release to allow all of the steam to escape until the valve drops.

5. Take out the lid and get rid of bay leaves.

6. Shred beef into bite-sized pieces using two forks. Toss the beef well in the juices to soak them up.

7. You can serve while still warm or chill in a sealed container for a maximum of 3 days or place in a freezer for a maximum of 3 months.

Cooking tips: You can use any cut of beef you prefer. In case you want to cook in a slow cooker, slow cook all ingredients for about 8 hours on low or 4 to 5 hours on high until beef becomes tender and easily shreds with a fork.

10. INSTANT POT GARLIC AND HERB PORK TENDERLOIN WITH CARROTS AND PEARL ONIONS

Preparation Time: 5 minutes | Cooking Time: 25 minutes | Serves: 4

Ingredients

- 1.5 lbs. Smithfield Roasted Garlic & Herb Fresh Pork Loin Filet
- 2 tablespoons cornstarch
- 1 tablespoon grapeseed oil
- 1 lb. baby carrots
- 1 cup pearl onions, frozen
- 1 cup water, divided

Instructions

1. Hit the sauté function on the instant pot. Once the pot displays hot, add in grapeseed oil. Chop Smithfield Roasted Garlic & Herb Fresh Pork Loin Filet in half using kitchen shears. Add pork loin filet into pot. Then sear for 8 minutes on all sides while flipping after a few minutes.

2. After the pork attains a lovely crust on the outside, take out and transfer onto a plate. Add in 1/2 cup of water, pearl onions, and baby carrots. Scrape off the brown bits from the pot's bottom with a wooden spoon. Combine for a minute. Put Smithfield Roasted Garlic & Herb Fresh Pork Loin Filets atop the onion/carrot mixture.

3. Cover pot with lid, seal and ensure the valve is set to the sealing position. Hit cancel. Set manual to 7 minutes. Once time is up, natural release the pressure for 7 minutes. Gently release any remaining steam before removing the lid.

4. Transfer the carrots, pork, and onions onto a plate. Press sauté and leave the broth to boil. As the broth is simmering, combine cornstarch and the remaining one cup of water together to form a slurry. Then whisk in cornstarch slurry inside the pot. Whisk until the gravy becomes thick. Flip the Pot.

5. Chop the pork loin filet into pieces of 1-inch thick. Add gravy on top and then serve together with onions and carrots. Enjoy right away.

11. INSTANT POT PEPPER BEEF

Preparation Time: 10 minutes | Cooking Time: 25 minutes | Serves: 2

Ingredients

- 2 tablespoons hoisin sauce
- 1 lb. skirt steak or stir fry beef
- 5 tablespoons soy sauce
- 1 red bell pepper, chopped into quarters
- 1 green bell pepper, chopped into quarters
- 1 teaspoon fresh ginger
- 3 tablespoons brown sugar
- 1 bundle spring onion, chopped into quarters
- 1 tablespoon garlic, minced

Instructions

1. Cut the spring onions and bell peppers. Reserve.

2. Into the instant pot, add beef along with one tablespoon soy sauce and 3/4 cup of water. Cook for 20 minutes at high pressure. When time is up, quick release the pressure after 5 minutes.

3. Drain the juice from the beef.

4. Combine together hoisin sauce, brown sugar, ginger, soy sauce and garlic. Mix thoroughly.

5. Into the instant pot, add spring onions and bell peppers and then set pot to sauté function. Stir fry the veggies and beef for around 3 minutes.

6. Add the sauce and let to cook for about 3 to 5 minutes until the sauce caramelizes around beef.

7. You can serve together with steamed white rice alongside chives from spring onions.

12. COUNTRY STYLE INSTANT POT CUBE STEAK RECIPE

Preparation Time: 10 minutes | Cooking Time: 30 minutes | Serves: 6

Ingredients

- 1 dry package of Lipton Onion Soup mix
- 2 lbs. cube steak
- 2 tablespoons oil
- 1/3 cup flour
- 2 cups beef broth
- 10.5 oz. can cream of celery soup
- 2 onions

Instructions

1. Start by chopping cube steak into smaller pieces.

2. Pour flour into ziplock bag.

3. Place steak one at a time into the bag to mix with flour.

4. Pour oil into the Instant Pot and press the sauté function.

5. Working in batches, place the cube steak into Instant Pot. Let to cook on each side until crispy and browned.

6. Reserve the cube steak. Use 3 tablespoons of beef broth to deglaze the pots' bottom.

7. Add the onions and let them cook until tender.

8. Place the cube steak atop onions.

9. Combine the remaining broth, Lipton onion soup mix and cream of celery soup.

10. Spread the sauce mixture on top of cube steak.

11. Let to cook for 20 minutes on manual high.

12. Do a quick release.

13. Switch off the instant pot and let to stand for 5 minutes. (This will make the gravy to thicken). Serve together with mashed potatoes or atop of rice.

13. INSTANT POT KOREAN PORK CHOPS

Preparation Time: 10 minutes | Cooking Time: 40 minutes | Serves: 2-6

Ingredients

- 2 to 6 small pork chops or pork steaks
- 3 to 6 teaspoons sriracha sauce, more for spicy and less for mild
- 1 tablespoon olive oil
- 3 teaspoons sesame oil
- 6 tablespoons honey
- ¾ cup soy sauce
- 2 tablespoons corn starch
- 5 to 6 tablespoons prepared minced garlic or 6 to 8 cloves minced garlic
- Black pepper and salt as desired
- 3 teaspoons fresh minced ginger

Instructions

1. Add oil into the pot and heat on sauté

2. Add pepper and salt to the pork chops

3. Working in batches, sauté the pork chops on each side for about 3 minutes per side until browned.

4. Whisk together the sriracha sauce soy sauce, garlic, ginger, honey and sesame oil in a medium size bowl.

5. Put the pork chops inside the Instant pot and then add the sauce to cover.

6. Cook for 12 minutes at high pressure.

7. Natural release the pressure for at least 14 minutes.

8. Take out the chops and reserve.

9. Make a slurry by combining water with corn starch.

10. Hit the sauté button on the pot and then whisk in cornstarch slurry.

11. Let to simmer while stirring for about 2 minutes until thickened.

12. Spread the sauce on top of pork chops and then serve.

14. LAZY DAY BEEF STEW (FRESH OR FROZEN BEEF)

Preparation Time: 20 minutes | Cooking Time: 45 minutes | Serves: 4

Ingredients

- 3 - 4 red-skinned potatoes, chopped into 1 inch pieces
- 1 large onion chopped
- 1 tablespoon vinegar
- 1 1/2 cup chicken or beef broth
- 3 cloves minced garlic
- 2 tablespoons soy sauce
- 1 tablespoon brown sugar
- 1 teaspoon salt
- 1 - 1.5 lbs. stew beef, fresh or frozen
- 1/2 teaspoon pepper
- 3 tablespoons water
- 2 to 3 carrots, chopped into 1 inch pieces
- 2 tablespoons cornstarch
- 1 cup peas, frozen
- 2 tablespoons sliced fresh parsley, if desired

Instructions

1. Into the instant pot, mix the first 10 ingredients. Cover the pot with lid and ensure the valve is moved to the sealing position. Hit the pressure cook button and set the time to 25 minutes.

2. As the content cook, chop the carrots and potatoes into 1 inch pieces (with skins on or peeled). Mix water with cornstarch until smooth to make a slurry.

3. When the time is up, you will hear beeps. Natural release for 10 minutes. Move the valve to the venting position to quick release the remaining pressure. Then open the pot when the pin drops.

4. Mix in the carrots and potatoes (excluding peas) and then gently press them into the liquid. Cover the pot with lid once again, then press the pressure cook button and set the time to 4 minutes. Once done, quick release and uncover the pot when the pin drops.

5. Press cancel and then sauté. Stir the cornstarch slurry and once stew boils, mix in approximately ½ the slurry. Boil to thicken it. If you prefer a thicker mix, add extra slurry.

6. Press cancel and mix in frozen peas. The stew's heat will eventually cook them without turning them to mush. Check the taste and add pepper and salt if necessary. If using, add parsley.

15. INSTANT POT BBQ PULLED PORK

Preparation Time: 10 minutes | Cooking Time: 45 minutes | Serves: 6

Ingredients

- 6 hamburger buns for serving
- 3 pound pork shoulder, chopped into four large chunks
- 4 tablespoons apple cider vinegar
- 2 1/2 cups bbq sauce
- 1 can coca cola may sub dry pepper or root beer
- 1/3 cup brown sugar
- 1 teaspoon onion powder
- 2 teaspoons garlic powder

Instructions

Pressure cooker/Instant Pot

1. Place pork into an instant pot that is lightly greased. Spread coca cola on top of pork.

2. Mix together onion powder, 2 cups bbq sauce, apple cider vinegar, brown sugar and garlic powder. Spread on top of pork.

3. Cover the pot with lid and ensure it's at the lock position. Set to cook for 45 minutes. Then natural release for ten minutes. Move the valve to vent position. Remove the lid when the float valve drops.

4. Shred pork into small chunks with 2 forks. Transfer the pork to a bowl using a slotted spoon (get rid of liquid from the pot) and then mix the remaining half cup of bbq sauce together with shredded pork.

5. You can serve the pulled pork over hamburger buns. If desired, you can sandwich the toppings to take the pulled pork to a higher level: Cole slaw, mayo, and extra bbq sauce.

Slow Cooker

1. Follow the same directions for cooking in Instant Pot but use a slow cooker. Cover the cooker and let to cook for 6 hours on low prior to shredding the pork.

Cooking tips

It's better to use bbq sauce with two different flavors like sweet and spicy or sweet and smoky. Using two kinds of bbq sauce together adds flavor to pork. You should increase the pressure cooking time to 1 hour 20 minutes to have a well cooked and very tender pork if using frozen pork that has not been chopped into four chunks.

16 INSTANT POT ITALIAN SAUSAGE TORTELLINI

Preparation Time: 15 minutes | Cooking Time: 5 minutes | Serves: 6

Ingredients

- 1 yellow diced onion
- 1 pound ground Italian sausage
- 19 oz. (1 package) frozen cheese tortellini
- 1 cup water or beef broth
- 1/2 cup half and half
- 28 oz. (1 can) crushed tomatoes
- 1/2 cup grated mozzarella cheese, if desired

Instructions

2. Switch the Instant Pot to the sauté function. Once hot sign is displayed, add sausage. Use a wooden spoon to break it up and then add diced onion.

3. When the onion becomes soft and the sausage turns brown, pour in water or beef broth. Then deglaze the pot.

4. Evenly spread the frozen tortellini on top. Evenly dump tomatoes on top of tortellini. Do not stir.

5. Close the lid and secure it. Ensure the valve is set to the sealing position. Adjust the pressure cook button to zero minutes.

6. Once done, allow the pot stand for five minutes. Push valve to venting position and then take out the lid.

7. Mix in half and half.

8. Transfer onto bowls and plates and then drizzle each serving with 1 1/2 tablespoons mozzarella cheese if desired.

17. INSTANT POT BEEF & CHEESY POTATOES

Preparation Time: 20 minutes | Cooking Time: 13 minutes | Serves: 1

Ingredients

- 6 large potatoes, uncooked
- 1.5 lbs. ground beef
- 2 cups shredded cheddar cheese
- 1 tablespoon Italian seasoning
- 3/4 C. chicken broth
- Cooking Spray
- 1 teaspoon paprika
- 1/4 teaspoon pepper
- 1/2 teaspoon salt

Instructions

1. Set the pot to the sauté function and then brown the ground beef.

2. In a small bowl, mix all the spices together. Combine well.

3. Cut the potatoes into ¼ inch thick pieces.

4. Into the pot, spread a layer of ⅓ of chopped potatoes and ground beef and add ⅓ of shredded cheese on top. Drizzle ⅓ of seasoning on top.

5. Repeat this two more times.

6. After layering, add the chicken broth.

7. Cover the pot with lid and seal the valve. Set to cook at high pressure for 13 minutes.

8. When time is up, release the pressure and then serve.

SOUPS AND STEWS

1. THE BEST INSTANT POT DETOX LENTIL VEGETABLES SOUP

Preparation Time: 10 minutes | Cooking Time: 15 minutes | Serves: 8

Ingredients

- ½ tablespoon olive oil
- 1 large zucchini chopped into 1-inch pieces
- 1 cup Lal Masoor / Red Lentils
- 4-7 cups water
- 5 large tomatoes chopped roughly
- 1 cup cauliflower florets chopped into small pieces
- 4 large garlic cloves finely chopped
- 2 teaspoon turmeric
- 1 large onion peeled and sliced into 1-inch pieces
- 1 cup broccoli florets chopped into small pieces
- 2 large carrots peeled and chopped into 1-inch pieces
- ¼ -1/2 teaspoon smoked paprika or chili powder to taste
- 1 ½ teaspoon salt
- 4 to 5 cleaned stalks celery and chopped into 1-inch pieces
- 1 small finely chopped ginger

Instructions

Preparation for soup

1. Clean the red lentils under cold water until the water runs clear. Then soak the lentils in water until when ready to use. In the meantime, clean all the veggies. Peel, wash and cut the veggies as directed in the ingredients list. Drain the lentils when ready to use.

Cooking on sauté setting

1. Put the inside pot into the instant pot, plug in the instant pot and then set to the sauté mode. Pour in oil when the screen displays the hot sign. Add garlic, ginger and onion into pot. Let to sauté for two minutes until the onions are soft a bit.

2. Add the cauliflower florets, zucchini, carrots and celery into the instant pot. Let to cook for 2 more minutes. Add red lentils, tomatoes, broccoli, red chili powder, salt and turmeric.

Stir well and then pour in 7 cups of water to have a very soupy consistency. For a lesser thicker consistency, add just 4 cups of water and use the same seasonings. Add salt to taste and stir. Turn off the sauté mode setting.

Manual/pressure cook method

1. Cover the instant pot with the lid and put the valve to no venting position. Push manual button and switch it to more plus high pressure. For slightly texture soup, set time to three minutes. For mushy texture, set time to 5 minutes. For no texture soup, you can cook for ten minutes. If you like a stew type of soup, cook for 5 minutes.

2. When the timer is done, natural release the pressure. Open the pot and then serve while still warm.

The traditional pressure cooker method

1. Follow the directions of cooking of the sautéing mode and adding the ingredients. Cook under pressure for one whistle. Decrease heat and let to cook for ten minutes with weight/whistle on. Switch off after minutes elapse and then open once the pressure is released.

Stovetop pot/pan cooking method

1. Follow the directions of the sautéing mode. Pour in water and heat to boil. Then decrease the heat and let to cook for approximately 30 to 35 minutes until the soup appears creamy and thick.

2. INSTANT POT MACARONI AND CHEESE

Preparation Time: 15 minutes | Cooking Time: 10 minutes | Serves: 8

Ingredients

- 1 cup Monterey jack cheese
- 4 cups water
- 1 teaspoon hot sauce
- 1 pound cheddar cheese
- 1 tablespoon dry mustard powder
- 1 pound pasta, gluten free
- 1 cup milk or half and half
- 2 tablespoons butter

Instructions

1. Add the following into the instant pot, hot sauce, dry mustard, pasta and water. Then pressure cook the contents for four minutes. Quick release on the pasta. In case the pot spits out a milky liquid, wait for about four to five minutes before you do a quick release.

2. You can drain the pasta if necessary and then return it into the pot.

3. Mix in hot sauce, milk, cheese and butter and stir until cheese has melted. Serve right away.

3. INSTANT POT CREAMY TORTELLINI, SPINACH AND CHICKEN SOUP

Preparation Time: 15 minutes | Cooking Time: 15 minutes | Serves: 8

Ingredients

- 1 ½ lbs. chicken breasts or chicken thighs, boneless and skinless
- 2 tablespoon tomato paste
- 14.5 oz. (2) cans petite diced tomatoes along with juices
- ½ cup parmesan cheese
- 4 cups chicken broth
- 1 tablespoon dried basil
- 2 teaspoon olive oil
- 2 cloves minced garlic
- ½ teaspoon pepper
- ½ teaspoon salt
- 1 cup warmed half and half
- 3 cups packed spinach, optional, you can use kale
- 1 medium and diced yellow onion
- 4 cups frozen cheese tortellini

Instructions

1. Switch the pot to the highest setting of sauté function. Add oil into the pot and heat. Then place in diced onion and stir for several minutes. Stir in garlic and cook for a few minutes until onions become translucent.

2. Pour in chicken broth, tomato paste, tomatoes, basil, chicken, pepper and salt. Stir and then cover with a lid. Ensure the valve is at the seal position. Push the pressure cook button and set the time to 15 minutes to cook at high pressure. When you hear a beep sound, release the pressure by slowly switching the valve to venting position.

3. Scoop out the chicken and transfer it onto a cutting board. Chop chicken into small pieces and return to pot. Mix in half and half, spinach, tortellini and parmesan cheese. Switch the pot to sauté so as to heat up the contents. After tortellini has warmed through, transfer the soup into bowls and then serve.

4. LIFE CHANGING INSTANT POT BEEF STEW

Preparation Time: 10 minutes | Cooking Time: 40 minutes | Serves: 5 to 6

Ingredients

- 2 tablespoons tapioca, small
- 2 lbs. chuck roast, fat trimmed beef chopped into one to two inch pieces
- 1 tablespoon sugar
- 1 medium onion, chopped thinly
- 1/2 cup tomato juice
- 6 carrots, chopped diagonally in thick pieces
- 2 teaspoons salt
- 2 stalks celery, chopped diagonally in thick pieces

Instructions

1. Instant pot directions: Into the pot, add all the ingredients. Switch pot to the setting for stew/meat and cook on high pressure for around 35 minutes. Once done, allow to mellow out for around ten minutes prior to releasing steam. Generally, everything is cooked through at this point but you can do a quick browning in your oven.

2. Traditional oven directions: Start by preheating the oven to 320 degrees F. Put all the ingredients into a ceramic or glass baking dish. You can also use a casserole dish of between 9x13 and 8x8. Use foil to cover the dish and then bake for about 3 to 4 hours. Add some water to gravy in case it dries out to loosen it prior to serving.

3. Completing in oven: Irrespective of preparing this recipe in the instant pot or oven, you can finish by heating in your hot oven for about 10 to 20 minutes at 400 degrees without covering. Serve. The meat will caramelize at the top and also helps to thicken the gravy.

Cooking tips

1. You can omit tapioca pearls to have a less thick gravy and will still be tasty.

2. Mix beef with 1/3 cup of flour and then shake to remove excess before transferring to the pot. For newer pots, add more liquid like a second can of tomato juice to prevent the burn warning on your pot.

3. You can prepare a slurry by mixing ¼ cup of water with 2 tablespoons of corn starch. Pour the slurry over the contents in the pot after cooking.

5. SPICY INSTANT POT CARROT SOUP

Preparation Time: 10 minutes | Cooking Time: 20 minutes | Serves: 4 to 6

Ingredients

- 1 14-ounce can coconut milk
- 1 chopped onion
- 8 to 10 large carrots, peeled and coarsely chopped
- 1/4 cup peanut butter
- 3 cloves peeled garlic
- 1 1/2 cups vegetable or chicken broth
- 1 tablespoon red curry paste
- Peanuts and cilantro for topping
- salt to taste

Instructions

1. Stovetop directions: Start by sautéing garlic and onions with little amount of oil until soft. Pour in curry paste, broth, coconut milk and carrots. Let to simmer until the carrots become soft. Stir in peanut butter until melted. Then blend in a blender until the resulting mixture is smooth. Generously add salt and then add cilantro and peanuts on top.

2. Instant pot directions: Into the pot, put all the ingredients and then adjust to 15 minutes. Once done, leave to cool for several minutes and then blend the mixture in a blender until smooth. Generously add salt and then add cilantro and peanuts on top.

Tip: You can add additional broth as required to have the desired silky smooth consistency.

6. CREAMY THAI COCONUT CHICKEN SOUP

Preparation Time: 5 minutes | Cooking Time: 6 minutes | Serves: 4

Ingredients

- 2 lbs. chicken thighs or chicken breast without bones and skin, cubed
- 2 1/2 tablespoons lime juice
- 2 tablespoons oil
- 3/4 cup coconut milk
- 1 small onion, chopped into quarters
- 1 red bell pepper, chopped into thick strips
- 1 tablespoon sugar
- 6 slices galangal, if using
- Cilantro leaves
- 3 cups chicken broth
- 2 tablespoons Thai red curry paste, Mae Ploy brand
- 2 tablespoons salt or fish sauce to taste
- 6 kaffir lime leaves, bruised and torn, if using

Instructions

1. Set the instant pot to the sauté setting. Add onion and then sauté for ten seconds prior to adding chicken. Sauté again the surface of the chicken becomes white. Add kaffir leaves (if using), bell peppers, Thai curry paste and galangal. Combine the contents thoroughly. Add sugar, fish sauce and chicken broth. Cover the instant pot and set to high pressure for six minutes.

2. Quick release once the pot beeps. Uncover carefully once the valve drops. Add to the soup, lime juice and coconut milk. Combine well. Drizzle cilantro on top and then serve right away.

Note: if it's hard to find kaffir lime leaves and galangal in your local Asian store, you can use lemongrass instead and omit the two ingredients. Lemongrass isn't a replacement for both kaffir lime leaves and galangal but it enhances the soup with its aroma and fragrance.

7. INSTANT POT COPYCAT PANERA BAKED POTATO SOUP

Preparation Time: 5 minutes | Cooking Time: 30 minutes | Serves: 4

Ingredients

- 1 cup heavy cream or whole milk
- 1 teaspoon olive oil
- 4 cups chicken broth
- 1/4 teaspoon white pepper
- 1 8 ounce packages cream cheese, chopped into chunks
- 4 cups potatoes, peeled and cubed
- 1/4 teaspoon ground black pepper
- 1/2 teaspoon seasoning salt
- 1 small onion, sliced

Instructions

1. Set the pot to the sauté mode.

2. Pour in oil and add onion. Cook for about 1 minute until translucent.

3. Add the potatoes and broth seasons.

4. Let to cook for 10 minutes on high pressure or you can use soup button.

5. Natural release the pressure (release any remaining steam after 15 minutes of natural release)

6. Set to the sauté function.

7. Mash some of the potatoes and then add cream cheese.

8. Stir to melt the cream cheese.

9. Place in heavy cream and stir to mix.

10. Serve right away with bacon bits, shredded cheese, chives, etc.

8. INSTANT POT BEEF BARLEY VEGETABLE SOUP

Preparation Time: 20 minutes | Cooking Time: 35 minutes | Serves: 10

Ingredients

- 1/3 cup rinsed pearl barley
- 1 sliced yellow onion
- 2 tablespoon vegetable oil or olive oil
- 1 lb. chopped potatoes (about two cups)
- 1 lb. stew meat or chuck roast (chop into 1 1/2-2 inch chunks)
- 1 cup chopped celery
- 2 chopped carrots
- 4 sprigs of fresh thyme (or 3/4 teaspoon dried)
- 3 minced garlic cloves
- 2 cups of fresh chopped tomatoes or 1 14.5 oz. can of diced tomatoes along with juice
- 2 bay leaves,
- 8 oz. chopped cabbage (around two cups)

- 3 cups beef or chicken broth, low in sodium
- 1 teaspoon black pepper
- 1 1/2 teaspoon salt

Instructions

1. Switch Instant Pot to sauté (or browning) mode. Add the oil once pot becomes hot.
2. Spread a single layer of the beef chunks on the bottom of pot. Cook for a few minutes to form a crust.
3. Flip beef over and brown on the other side.
4. Add celery, carrots and onion. Mix and then scrape up the brown bits on the pot's bottom.
5. Mix in garlic and let to cook for 1 minute.
6. Add tomatoes along with juice, broth, barley, potatoes, thyme, cabbage, pepper, salt, and bay leaves. Stir.
7. Cover the pot with lid and then move the steam release valve to the seal position.
8. Press the cancel button. Press the stew/soup button (or manual/ pressure cook) to cook for 20 minutes. (Since the pot is full, it will take a few minutes to come to pressure)
9. Once cooking cycle completes, allow pot to naturally release pressure for about 15 minutes. Open lid after the pin in the lid has dropped. Then stir the soup. Get rid of the bay leaves.
10. Serve right away.

Recipe Notes

If you are Gluten-Free, leave out the barley.

9. CORN CHOWDER (OR CORN AND CRAB)

Preparation Time: 10 minutes | Cooking Time: 20 minutes | Serves: 4

Ingredients

- 1 lb. diced potatoes
- 1/4 cup to 1 cup heavy cream
- 1/2 cup red bell pepper, diced
- 2 slices bacon, diced, if desired
- 2 tablespoon cornstarch, if desired
- 3/4 cup diced carrots
- 1 teaspoon salt
- 1 teaspoon sugar
- 1/2 teaspoon fresh thyme, chopped
- 1 large diced onion
- 1/2 to 2 teaspoon hot sauce to taste
- 1/2 cup celery, diced
- 3 tablespoon water, if desired
- 4 cups chicken broth
- 3 cups fresh or frozen corn

- 1/2 teaspoon pepper
- Cooked crab meat, if desired no specific amounts

Instructions

1. Set pot to sauté mode. Add bacon if using after the display shows hot. Let to cook until almost crisp. Add red pepper, celery, onion, and carrot. (If not adding bacon, add two tablespoons of butter.) Then sauté for about 2 or 3 minutes. Press the cancel button and pour in the broth.

2. Deglazing the Instant pot: Thoroughly scrape off all browned bits from the pot's bottom into the liquid. Add thyme, potatoes, hot sauce, pepper and salt. Cover the pot.

3. Be sure the valve is at the seal position. Set to pressure cook or manual for 6 minutes.

4. Once time is up, move the valve to the venting position to quick release. Once the pin has dropped, push the cancel button and remove the lid.

5. Press the sauté button and then add sugar and corn. Heat to boil and then let to simmer for 1 to 2 minutes. Break up some of the potatoes with a potato masher. For a thicker chowder, mix water and cornstarch together and then add about ½ of the mix while stirring continuously. You can add more if you prefer a very thick chowder.

6. In case you're adding crab, add it in now and stir. Cook for 1 minute to heat the crab and then push the cancel button.

7. Add your desired amount of cream from 1/4 to 1 full cup. Check the taste and add pepper and salt if necessary. Serve together with a garnish of red peppers or bacon bits or anything else you prefer.

10. INSTANT POT DILL PICKLE SOUP

Preparation Time: 15 minutes | Cooking Time: 5 minutes | Serves: 4-6

Ingredients

- 1/4 tsp white pepper
- 1 cup diced dill pickles
- 5 cups vegetable or chicken broth, low sodium)
- 2 cups finely diced carrot
- 7 tablespoon unsalted butter
- 2 medium peeled baking potatoes, chopped into 1 inch pieces

To finish

- 1/4 cup flour (for thickening, if desired)
- 1 cup dill pickle juice (add 1/4 cup at a time)
- Heavy cream to suit your taste
- Salt to suit your taste

Tools needed

- Immersion Blender
- 6 quart or 8 quart pressure cooker

Instructions

1. Add all of the ingredients into the instant pot apart from flour, heavy cream, salt and pickle juice.
2. Cover the pot with lid and move the steam release valve to the sealing position. Set to pressure cook/manual for five minutes at high pressure.
3. After cooking is done, leave the pot to stand without disturbing for ten minutes (ten minute natural release). Do a controlled quick release by moving steam release valve to the vent position, in short bursts until you're sure that it's only steam that will spew out of the vent and not soup due to pressure.
4. Blend the soup with an immersion blender. You can also blend in a blender in small batches or use a potato masher to mash it.
5. Check the taste and feel free to add more pickle juice, 1/4 cup at a time until you get the desired pickle flavor. If desired, add salt (you can add 1/4 teaspoon).
6. For a thicker soup
7. Combine 1/4 cup of the cream and 1/4 cup of flour together (stir well to get rid of lumps). Set the pot to the sauté setting and mix in the mixture. Mix until it has thickened. For a very thick soup add more (although it should not be very thick). Switch the pot off and then serve.
8. If desired, complete with cream to suit your taste. You can garnish with it.

11. GINSENG GOJI CHICKEN SOUP

Preparation Time: 20 minutes | Cooking Time: 40 minutes | Serves: 3-4

Ingredients

- 2 (about 28 gm) American ginseng, dried
- 5 cups water
- ½ (about 710 gm) chicken
- 15 gm goji berries (also known as wolfberry)
- 3 slices ginger
- 15 gm dried red dates, deseeded
- 2 candied dates
- 35 gm white lotus seeds

Instant Pot Method:

1. Start by steaming the dried ginseng for about ten minutes or until soft to chop. Rinse and then drain all the other ingredients. Reserve.

2. Rinse chicken and then chop into 2-3 large chunks. Remove blood and other impurities by blanching in boiling water. Then rinse and drain thoroughly.

3. Transfer chicken chunks along with all the other ingredients into the Instant Pot, candied dates, ginseng, lotus seeds, ginger, and goji. Add in water.

4. Cover with the lid and ensure the steam release knob is at the sealing position. Press soup button and cook for 35 minutes at high pressure. Press the cancel button and then do a quick release. Take out the lid. Press the sauté button and let to cook for ten minutes. Add salt to taste and then serve while still hot.

Stove-top Method:

- Follow the instant pot instructions above on how to prepare the ingredients.

- Transfer all ingredients into a large pot. Add in 6 to 6½ cups water and heat to boil on high heat. Decrease the heat to medium-low and let to simmer for about 2 to 2½ hours. Add salt to taste and then serve while still hot.

Cooking tips: Feel free to remove chicken skin prior to cooking to make the soup less greasy. You can use an oil filter to filter out oil on sauce or soup surface. Look for American ginseng at Chinese herbal medicine stores or Asian grocers. Request the staff at any Chinese herbal medicine shop to assist you in slicing ginseng or just go for the sliced ones.

12. BROCCOLI CHEDDAR SOUP

Preparation Time: 10 minutes | Cooking Time: 20 minutes | Serves: 2

Ingredients

- 5 cups chicken or vegetable broth or water
- 1 medium onion, sliced
- 1 - 2 stalks celery thinly chopped
- 2 cloves crushed garlic, if desired
- 1 lb. broccoli, chopped in large chunks
- 1 teaspoon salt
- 1/2 teaspoon pepper
- 2 teaspoon fresh basil or 1 teaspoon dried basil, if desired
- 1 teaspoon sugar if desired to enhance the flavor
- 1/4 cup flour
- 1 - 2 cup cups grated sharp cheddar
- 2/3 cup Water
- 1/2 cup milk, heavy cream and Half & Half.

Instructions

1. Transfer the first eight ingredients into the Instant Pot and cover with lid. Move the valve to the sealing position and set to pressure cook for 5 minutes.

2. As the contents cook, whisk water and flour together until smooth completely. Once the pot beeps, move the valve from the sealing to the venting position. Once pin has dropped, push the cancel button and take out the lid.

3. Set the pot to sauté mode and heat to boil while stirring often. Whisk the flour/water slurry and transfer about ½ of it to the soup while stirring until it starts to boil and thickens. To make it thicker, you can add some more slurry and let to boil after each addition.

4. Puree the soup with an immersion blender, food processor or blender. Transfer the soup back into the pot.

5. Press the cancel button and then add cheese (for an extra kick, you can add some Parmesan). Mix until smooth and melted. Avoid boiling after adding cheese. Add sugar and milk/cream. Check the taste and season with pepper and salt as desired. Serve together with a drizzle of grated cheese, croutons or broccoli florets.

13. INSTANT POT BEEF AND BARLEY STEW

Preparation Time: 10 minutes | Cooking Time: 45 minutes | Serves: 6

Ingredients

- 1.5 lbs. lean beef stew meat
- 1 diced onion
- 2 teaspoon flour
- 6 cups beef broth
- 3/4 teaspoon thyme
- 2 cups hash brown potatoes
- 2 teaspoon olive oil
- 2 bay leaves
- 1 cup diced celery
- 1 cup diced carrots
- 2 tablespoon tomato paste
- 2/3 cup rinsed pearl barley
- 4 diced garlic cloves

Instructions

1. Switch the Instant Pot to the sauté setting. Add the oil when the pot becomes hot. Mix the beef with pepper, flour, and salt. Transfer to the pot and then brown on each side for around 5 to 7 minutes. It's better to work in 2 batches so as to get a more intense flavor because beef will brown more. Take out the beef and reserve.

2. Add carrots, onions, and celery. Let to cook for about 4 to 5 minutes. Add garlic and tomato paste. Let to cook for about 1 minute until fragrant.

3. Add the pearl barley, beef, bay leaves, beef broth, and thyme. Combine together.

4. Cover the pot and then press the button for soup/stew and set time to 25 minutes. Natural release the pressure when cooking is done. Remove cover and then add potatoes. Cook for five minutes until the potatoes are warmed up. Add pepper and salt to taste.

5. Cooking with slow cooker: Follow the above steps 1 and 2 and use a large pan. Then transfer those ingredients into slow cooker together with barley, thyme, broth, and bay leaves. Let to cook for 8 hours on low. Mix in potatoes and cook for ten more minutes or until the potatoes are warmed through. Add pepper and salt to taste.

14. PERFECT INSTANT POT BEEF STEW

Preparation Time: 20 minutes | Cooking Time: 20 minutes | Serves: 6-8

Ingredients

- 2 cups frozen peas
- 1 tablespoon oil
- 6 ounce can tomato paste
- 1/2 cup white or yellow onions, chopped
- 2 to 2 1/2 cups potatoes (any variety), peeled and chopped, approximately 1/2-inch pieces
- 3 cups beef broth, low-sodium
- 2-3 pounds stew meat, or arm roast or chuck, trimmed and chopped into one inch cubes
- 2 tablespoons tapioca, instant/minute
- 3 tablespoons soy sauce
- 1/4 teaspoon black pepper, you can use coarsely ground
- 2 to 2 1/2 cups carrots, chopped, approximately 1/2-inch pieces
- 2 bay leaves

Instructions

1. Set the pot to the sauté mode and adjust the heat to the normal setting. Pour in oil and the onions and let to cook for about 2 to 3 minutes while stirring occasionally until onions begin to become translucent. Add tomato paste and stir it into the onions. Let to cook for about 1 to 2 minutes.

2. Add black pepper, beef broth, soy sauce, bay leaves and tapioca. Then stir or whisk to mix.

3. Add in stew meat and then stir. Close pot with lid and ensure the vent is at the closed position. Let to cook for 18 minutes on high pressure.

4. Once cooking is done, natural release the pressure for around ten minutes and then do a quick release to release the remaining pressure. Add potatoes and carrots. Dry the seal and inside of lid and ensure the ring is pushed downwards all the way (in case the ring is too wet or not in place, the instant pot might not come up to pressure again). Cover the pot with lid and ensure the vent is at the closed position. Let to cook for 3 minutes on high pressure.

5. Do a pressure quick release (or release naturally for ten minutes and then do quick release). Remove bay leaves. Mix in frozen peas and then add more pepper and salt as desired. Stew should thicken a little when cooling.

Cooking tips: You can use Worcestershire sauce in place of half of the soy sauce. In addition, you can chop the potatoes and carrots while the first round of ingredients are cooking in the pot.

Instant tapioca is also known as "granulated tapioca". Small or large pearl tapioca is different. It makes the stew thick without any odd flavors or textures. (Try with flour, cornstarch or subbing tapioca flour).

15. INSTANT POT SAUSAGE CHICKPEA STEW

Preparation Time: 10 minutes | Cooking Time: 16 minutes | Serves: 6

Ingredients

- 1 lb. chickpeas, dried and soaked overnight
- 1/2 teaspoon oregano
- 2 leaves bay leaf
- 28 oz. tomato sauce, diced
- 3 whole chopped chicken sausages
- 1 cup chicken broth
- 1 pinch sea salt and pepper to suit your taste
- 3 cups fresh cored and chopped kale,
- 1/4 teaspoon ground coriander
- 1/2 teaspoon paprika

Instructions

1. In a large bowl, put chickpeas and then add cold water to cover. Soak for about 12-24 hours. In case the level of water goes down, you can add more water to cover chickpeas.

2. The following day, drain the chickpeas and rinse. Transfer to the instant pot and then add cans of diced tomato sauce, seasonings, sausage and chicken broth. Cover the pot and move the vent knob to the lock position. Let to cook for 16 minutes on high pressure. Once done, natural release the pressure.

3. After pressure is released, remove the lid and place in the chopped kale. Toss to combine and ensure kale is submersed. Cover the pot again and allow to stand for five minutes prior to serving.

4. Before you serve, add the flavorful toppings such as muffin crumbs, grated parmesan cheese, herbs or anything you like.

16. SANDY'S INSTANT POT BEEF STEW

Preparation Time: 20 minutes | Cooking Time: 35 minutes | Serves: 6

Ingredients

- 2 tablespoon Worcestershire Sauce
- 4 Potatoes, chopped in 1 1/2 inch chunks
- 2 cups chicken or beef broth, low in sodium
- 4 carrots, chopped in 1 inch pieces
- 1/2 cup red wine or more broth
- 8 oz. small crimini mushrooms
- 3 tablespoons tomato paste
- 2 1/2 lbs. chuck roast, chopped into 1 1/2 inch cubes
- 1 1/2 teaspoons kosher salt
- 1 sprig fresh rosemary
- 3 minced garlic cloves
- 1 teaspoon sugar
- 2 ribs celery, sliced into 1 inch pieces
- 2 tablespoon red wine vinegar
- 3 sprigs fresh thyme
- 1 large onion, chopped into 1 inch pieces
- 1 bay leaf

For thickening after cooking

- 3 tablespoons softened butter
- 3 tablespoons flour

Instructions

1. Set the instant pot to the sauté mode.

2. Place the stainless inner liner on the base and then add Worcestershire sauce, broth, wine, and vinegar and tomato paste. Mix thoroughly. Heat the mixture on a low simmer.

3. Add all the other ingredients into the pot apart from the thickener. Mix and brown the meat.

4. Close with the lid and move the steam release valve to sealing position.

5. Press the cancel button.

6. Then press the stew/meat button and set to high pressure for 35 minutes.

7. It will take a few minutes to come to pressure because the pot is full.

8. Once cooking is done, natural release the steam for 15 minutes.

9. Release the remaining pressure manually. You should release the pressure in short bursts since a full release will cause hot stew to spew out of steam release valve and probably all over the kitchen.

10. Carefully open the pot's lid and face it away from you after the steam/pressure is released from the pot and pin in the lid has dropped.

11. Transfer the stew and not the liquid into a large serving bowl using a slotted spoon.

12. Set the pot to sauté function.

13. Combine butter and flour together for thickening. You can heat butter in microwave for five seconds to make it soft.

14. Whisk in the thickener once liquid begins to simmer and let to cook for a few minutes while stirring continuously until it begins to thicken.

15. Serve right away.

Cooking tips: In case you prefer browning the meat first, mix meat cubes with flour, switch pot to the sauté mode, then pour in some vegetable oil and brown all sides of meat before you continue.

EGGS AND VEGETABLES

1. INSTANT POT REFRIED BEANS

Preparation Time: 10 minutes | Cooking Time: 1 hour 10 minutes | Serves: 6

Ingredients

- 3 cups water
- 2 cups (1 pound) dry pinto beans
- 2 bay leaves
- 1/8 to ¼ tsp cayenne pepper, if desired
- 2 tsp extra-virgin olive oil
- 1 cored, seeded, and finely chopped jalapeno
- 1 tsp dried oregano
- 1 tsp ground cumin
- 4 cups vegetable stock or low-sodium chicken stock, divided
- 1 ½ tsp kosher salt
- 1 small yellow onion, sliced into ¼ inch pieces
- 3 cloves garlic, minced about 1 tbsp.
- For serving: shredded Monterey jack cheese or queso fresco, if desired, avocado, diced red onion, diced tomatoes, chopped fresh cilantro

Instructions

1. Into a large colander, put the pinto beans and then rinse them well. Pick over the beans and discard any damaged or deformed beans. Reserve the rinsed beans.

2. Set an instant pot of 6-quart or large to sauté. Pour in oil and then add jalapeno and onion when the oil is hot. Let to sauté for 2 minutes. Add garlic and cook for about 30 seconds until fragrant. Pour in some splashed of chicken stock and then scrape across the pot's bottom to remove any stuck bits of food to prevent a burn warning. Add cayenne, the remaining stock, the rinsed and drained beans, oregano, cumin, salt, bay leaves, and water. Stir lightly to mix.

3. Cover the pot with the lid and cook for 45 minutes on high. After 45 minutes of pressure cooking, allow the pressure to release naturally for 25 minutes. Then vent to remove the remaining pressure. Remove the lid carefully. The beans should be very syrupy.

4. Get rid of bay leaves. In a measuring cup or bowl, save two cups of the bean cooking liquid. Drain the remaining bean liquid. Place the beans back into the pot. Puree the beans

with a potato masher or an immersion blender while adding the reserved liquid as needed until they attain your desired consistency. (Alternatively, scoop the beans in a blender in batches and the puree. Make sure you allow the beans to first cool to prevent them from splattering.). Check the taste and adjust the seasoning. Drizzle with your favorite toppings and serve.

Cooking tips

You can chill or freeze the leftover beans for a maximum of three months.

To have easier portions: Cool the beans completely, divide them into ziptop freezer bags and label with a date. Squeeze out as much air as you can, press the beans such that the bag lays flat and then seal the bags. Freeze the bags while flat for easy storage. Leave beans to thaw in the fridge overnight, and then gently reheat atop the stove with a splash of stock or water as needed to thin the beans back out.

2. INSTANT POT GREEN BEANS

Preparation Time: 5 minutes | Cooking Time: 8 minutes | Serves: 2

Ingredients

- ½ cup cold water
- ½ pound green beans

Optional stir frying ingredients

- 4 minced garlic cloves
- 1 tablespoon olive oil or peanut oil
- Fish sauce and salt if desired

Instructions

1. Cooking green beans in pot: Add half cup of cold water and then put the steamer rack into the Instant Pot. Put the green beans on top of steamer rack. Then cook at low pressure for 0 to 2 minutes (0 minute if you want crunchy texture and 2 minutes for softer texture). Quick release the pressure.

2. You can serve the green beans. If serving at this step, you just need to add black pepper and salt to taste.

Optional Stir-Frying

1. If continuing with the stir-frying option, do not seasoning at this step. Just drain off the water and reserve the green beans to air dry.

2. Preparing the Instant Pot: Drain the hot water and then dry inner pot with towel. Then heat up the pot (push the sauté button, and set to the sauté more function). Make sure the pot is very hot before adding garlic (The pot's indicator should read hot).

3. Sautéing green beans and garlic: Pour 1 tablespoon olive oil or peanut oil into the pot. Be sure the oil has coated the entire bottom of pot. Place in the minced garlic and then sauté for about 30 seconds. Avoid burning the garlic. Add in the air-dried green beans and then sauté for about 30 seconds. Add to taste fish sauce (about 1.5 to 2 teaspoons) and fine sea salt. Sauté for 30 more seconds. At this point, garlic will be super flavorful and golden brown.

4. Serve the garlicy green beans right away.

3. INSTANT POT GARLIC PARMESAN WHOLE ROASTED CAULIFLOWER

Preparation Time: 2 minutes | Cooking Time: 1 minute | Serves: 1

Ingredients

- 2 tablespoons parmesan cheese
- 1 head of cauliflower
- 2 tablespoons chopped parsley
- 1 clove minced garlic
- 1/4 cup melted butter
- 1 teaspoon grated lemon zest
- 1/4 teaspoon ground black pepper
- 1/4 teaspoon salt

Instructions

1. Start by trimming the leaves from the cauliflower head and then clean. Transfer onto the trivet in the pot along with 1/2 to 1 cup water.

2. Mix parsley, butter, pepper, salt, garlic, and lemon zest. Rub the mixture over cauliflower and then slather well.

3. Cover pot with lid and be sure it's at the sealing position. Move the toggle to seal.

4. Press the pressure button (it will set to high pressure automatically). Adjust the timer to 1 minutes and press start. Once done, do a quick release.

To have an extra crispy finish

1. Gently take out the cauliflower head and transfer it to a baking sheet.

2. Drizzle with 2 tablespoons of Parmesan cheese on the sides and on top.

3. Transfer into an oven and broil until the cheese starts to brown.

4. EASY, PERFECT, FLUFFY INSTANT POT QUINOA

Preparation Time: 1 minute | Cooking Time: 1 minute | Serves: 1

Ingredients

- 2 to 1/2 cups vegetable stock or water
- 2 cups quinoa, rinsed in a fine-mesh sieve
- 1 teaspoon coconut oil or any other you prefer or omit oil

Instructions

1. Place quinoa in a fine-mesh strainer and then rinse with running water for several minutes.

2. Press the sauté button and when the pot is hot, pour in the rinsed quinoa, coconut oil and water.

3. Cover the pot with lid and ensure the valve is at the sealing position. Set to cook at high pressure for 1 minute.

4. Once cooking is done, do a natural pressure release for about 10 min.

5. Uncover the pot.

6. Use a fork to fluff quinoa and then serve.

5. INSTANT POT LENTIL CURRY

Preparation Time: 10 minutes | Cooking Time: 15 minutes | Serves: 4-6

Ingredients

- 3/4 teaspoon ground turmeric
- 1 1/2 cups green or brown lentils
- 1 cup and 1 tablespoon water, divided
- 14 ounces (1 can) light coconut milk
- 1 small finely shopped shallot
- 1 tablespoon curry powder and 1 teaspoon
- 1/2 tablespoon coconut oil
- 3 tablespoons fresh ginger, minced
- Chopped fresh cilantro, for serving
- 2 tablespoons minced garlic, around 6 cloves
- 1 teaspoon kosher salt
- Cooked brown rice, for serving
- 1/8 to 1/4 teaspoon cayenne pepper, can add more make it spicier or omit if desired
- 1/2 tablespoon brown sugar or coconut sugar
- 2 tablespoons freshly squeezed lemon juice, approximately 1/2 large lemon

Instructions

1. Start by rinsing the lentils and then drain. Reserve. Switch the instant pot to the sauté function and pour in coconut oil. When the oil melts, add garlic, ginger, the shallot, and 1 tablespoon of water. Cook while stirring occasionally for 2 minutes until the shallot is soft and very fragrant. Add cayenne, turmeric, salt, curry powder, and coconut sugar. Mix vigorously. Move back and do not inhale the steam from the pot because it will be spicy. Add the coconut milk, 1 cup of water and lentils. Mix to completely coat the lentils with the liquid.

2. Press the cancel button, seal the lid, and then set to cook for 15 minutes on high pressure. (It may take around 8 minutes for pressure to build and then the timer will start.) When time is up, natural release the pressure for 10 minutes and then vent to get rid of the remaining pressure. Uncover the pot and mix in lemon juice. Check the taste and season as desired. In case the curry becomes too thick, add some more water to make it loose. Serve while still hot along with rice, drizzled with cilantro.

Cooking tips

- You can transfer any leftovers into an airtight container and then store in the fridge for about 4 to 5 days or place in a freezer for about 2 to 3 months. Allow to thaw overnight in the fridge. Lentils will thicken as they cool and hence, before reheating, drizzle with some, water, coconut milk or chicken or vegetable stock. Gently rewarm on the stovetop or in a microwave while adding additional liquid as required.

- Try not to use yellow or red lentils in your Instant Pot because they have a delicate texture and they usually fall apart.

- To prepare on the stove: Cook lentils (feel free to use any kind of lentils you prefer). Over medium-high heat, sauté the spices, shallot, garlic and ginger as instructed in a separate large, rimmed skillet. Decrease the heat to low, and then add coconut sugar and coconut milk. Allow to simmer gently for about 4 to 5 minutes until thickened slightly. Mix in the coked lentils and lemon juice.

6. INSTANT POT CAULIFLOWER TIKKA MASALA

Preparation Time: 10 minutes | Cooking Time: 25 minutes | Serves: 4

Ingredients

- 1 28-ounce can (about 3 cups) diced tomatoes along with their juice
- 1 tablespoon oil or vegan butter
- 3 cloves of minced garlic
- 1/2 cup cashew cream or non-dairy yogurt
- 1 medium diced onion
- 1 teaspoon turmeric
- 1 tablespoon maple syrup
- 1/2 teaspoon ground chili
- 1 tablespoon freshly grated ginger
- 1/2 teaspoon salt
- 2 teaspoon dried fenugreek leaves
- 1/4 teaspoon ground cumin
- 1 small cauliflower head, chopped into florets (of approximately 4 cups florets)
- 2 teaspoon garam masala
- Toppings if desired: roasted cashews, fresh parsley

Instructions

1. Adjust the Instant Pot to the sauté function for seven minutes. Then pour in oil. When hot, add ginger, garlic and onion. Let to cook for about 3 to 4 minutes or until onions begin to become soft and caramelize. Add salt, cumin, chili, turmeric, garam masala and dried fenugreek leaves. Continue cooking for 2 more minutes while stirring often to ensure not burning. Pour in a few tablespoons of water, then scrape bottom to prevent sticking and this will prevent pot from displaying a "burn" sign.

2. Add cauliflower florets, maple syrup and crushed tomatoes. Cover the pot with lid and ensure the vent is at the sealing position. Hit the button for pressure cook and set the time to two minutes. The pot should take approximately ten minutes to come to pressure. Cook for 2 minutes under pressure.

3. When the time is up and you hear a beep sound, let to stand for a minute before releasing the pressure. Mix in non-dairy yogurt to combine.

4. You can serve while still hot with tofu, rice, or naan and topped with roasted cashews and fresh parsley if desired.

Cooking tips: You can add an extra teaspoon of ground chili for a spicier curry. Feel free to add half cup of water in case the diced tomatoes seem to not have much juice.

7. INSTANT POT STEEL CUT OATS

Preparation Time: 5 minutes | Cooking Time: 24 minutes | Serves: 6

Ingredients

- 4 to 5 cups water
- 2 cups steel cut oats (if need be, use certified gluten-free)

Instructions

1. Into the bowl of the Instant Pot, mix water with steel cut oats and stir well. You can use 5 cups of water for more of a porridge-like texture or 4 cups of water for thicker oats. Cover pot with lid and be sure to move the vent to the seal position.

2. Hit manual button and set the timer to four minutes on high pressure. The pot should start automatically.

3. Once the pot beeps, natural release the pressure for 20 minutes. (The pot's timer should remain on after the cooking time to show you how long it has been kept warm, unless you switch off the pot. You can keep it on for the timer function.)

4. After 20 minutes elapse, move vent to the venting position in order remove the remaining pressure. Gently take out the pot's lid and mix oats to incorporate the water that may have risen to the top. The oats should be look nice and thick and have a porridge-like texture.

5. Serve while still warm together with a splash of non-dairy milk, maple syrup, and cinnamon if desired. You can store the leftover oats in individual containers in the refrigerator for a maximum of one week for enjoy a fast breakfast when busy.

8. INSTANT POT PUMPKIN WALNUT CHILI

Preparation Time: 15 minutes | Cooking Time: 1 hour | Serves: 12

Ingredients

- 1 28-ounce can fire-roasted tomatoes
- 6 cups broth or water (refill tomato can around 2 times)
- ½ minced onion
- 2 chopped poblano peppers
- 3 cloves garlic, minced
- 1 tablespoons smoked paprika
- 2 to 3 chopped chipotle peppers
- 1 tablespoon salt
- 2 tablespoons chili powder
- 1 cup red lentils
- 2 cups chopped walnuts
- 1 cup bulgur

Add at the end:

- 2 or 3 14-ounce cans rinsed and drained black beans
- 1 14-ounce can pumpkin puree

Instructions

1. Start by placing all of the chili ingredients into the instant pot and then set to the soup mode (for about 30 minutes).

2. Once time is up, release the steam and then mix in black beans, pumpkin and add more spice, more salt, etc. You can serve with cornbread, avocado, cilantro, lime wedges, rice, tortilla chips or anything you prefer. In case it's too thick, thin it out by adding more broth or water.

9. INSTANT POT ALOO GOBI – CURRIED POTATO CAULIFLOWER

Preparation Time: 10 minutes | Cooking Time: 20 minutes | Serves: 4

Ingredients

- 1 small cauliflower, sliced into large florets
- 2 medium potatoes, cubed small
- 1/2 small onion
- 1/2 teaspoon turmeric
- 2 tomatoes
- 1 teaspoon ground cumin
- 6 to 7 cloves of garlic
- 1 teaspoon oil
- Cilantro, cayenne/pepper flakes, lemon and garam masala for garnish
- 1/2 teaspoon paprika
- 1/2 to 1 teaspoon garam masala
- 1/2 hot green chile
- 3/4 to 1 teaspoon salt
- 1 inch ginger

Instructions

1. Blend green chile, ginger, garlic, onion, and tomato until smooth.

2. Set the instant pot to sauté function. Once hot, pour oil into the pot. (You can place in half teaspoon of cumin seeds and let to cook until slightly darkened at this point.) Pour onion tomato puree into pot. Rinse blender with 1 to 2 tablespoons of water and pour into the pot.

3. Add potato and spices and combine thoroughly. Use a fitting glass lid to cover the pot and let to cook for about 4 to 5 minutes.

4. Place in cauliflower and stir thoroughly. Cover pot with lid and ensure you have sealed. Set the manual on low pressure for 2 minutes (preferred) or 0 minutes on high pressure. (0 mins or ½ whistle with the stove top pressure cooker).

5. Carefully do a quick release to release the pressure. Then add lemon juice, cayenne, cilantro and a drizzle of garam masala. Serve while still hot together with rice, flatbread, curries, or Dals.

Cooking tips

For stove top skillet: over medium heat, heat oil in a skillet and then add the spices and blended mixture from step 1. Let to cook for 3 to 4 minutes until garlic does not smell raw. Stir in potatoes, cover and let to cook for about 3 to 4 minutes. Mix in cauliflower. Cover the skillet and let to cook for ten minutes. Mix and if too dry, add water. Check the taste and adjust spice and salt. Continue cooking while covered for a few minutes until cooked to your liking.

For variations: You can replace garam masala with other spices such as 1/2 teaspoon of dried fenugreek leaves, 1/4 teaspoon of each pepper and cinnamon or 1/2 to 1 teaspoon of berbere or 2 teaspoons of panch phoron.

To make the dish a main course: You can add peas, greens, coconut milk after adding cauliflower. For garnish, add more garam masala. Serve together with whole grain flatbreads.

Cauliflower usually cooks very fast and hence, it's better to use large pieces. In case of overcooking the mixture, you should mash up everything and then add some vegan butter, chopped onion, lemon and garam masala. Then serve as pav bhaji or veggie mash.

10. INSTANT POT GARLIC PARMESAN WHOLE ROASTED BROCCOLI

Preparation Time: 5 minutes | Cooking Time: 1 minute | Serves: 10

Ingredients

- 2 tablespoons parmesan cheese
- 1 head of broccoli
- 1 clove minced garlic
- 2 tablespoons chopped parsley
- 1/4 teaspoon ground black pepper
- 1/4 cup melted butter
- 1/4 teaspoon salt
- 1 teaspoon grated lemon zest

Instructions

1. Start by trimming the leaves from the broccoli head and then wash. Transfer onto the trivet in the pot along with 1/2 - 1 cup of water. (You can form a bowl from tinfoil to hold melted butter and this makes it easy when transferring to cookie sheet for broiling) Mix butter, parsley, pepper, salt, garlic, and lemon zest. Rub the mixture over broccoli and slather well.

2. Cover with lid, ensure it is at the sealing position and then seal by turning the toggle.

3. Hit the pressure button (and pot should switch to high pressure automatically). Adjust the time to one minute and press start. Once done, quick release the pressure.

To have an extra crispy finish

1. Gently take out the broccoli head and transfer onto a baking sheet.

2. Drizzle with two tablespoons of Parmesan cheese on the sides and top.

3. Transfer to the oven to broil until the cheese begins to brown.

11. SCRAMBLED EGGS IN AN INSTANT POT

Preparation Time: 5 minutes | Cooking Time: 7 minutes | Serves: 2

Ingredients

- Pepper
- Salt
- About 1 tablespoon milk
- 2 eggs
- ½ tablespoon butter

Instructions

1. Use non-stick spray to spritz a small heat-proof bowl.

2. Crack the two eggs into the bowl.

3. Add pepper, milk and salt. Then use a fork to beat until uniform, more or less.

4. Add in butter.

5. Into the Instant pot, add one cup of water and place the trivet.

6. Place the bowl on top of the trivet, cover the pot and its steam vent.

7. Adjust the instant pot to Steam for 7 minutes at low pressure. Pot should begin chugging away heating the water. Begin counting down from seven minutes.

8. Once the timer is done, release the pressure right away and uncover the pot. Eggs will seem mostly cooked.

9. Check whether the eggs are cooked by stirring with a fork. Have no worries in case they seem a bit liquidly since they will continue cooking in bowl for 1 minute or so. In case they seem too undercooked, place back the lid and let to sit for 1 minute or so. They should be creamy and not really hard at the end.

10. Use a hot pad to take out the bowl and then use a fork to fluff the eggs. Serve immediately while hot.

12. INSTANT POT HARD BOILED EGGS

Preparation Time: 5 minutes | Cooking Time: 10 minutes | Serves: 8

Ingredients

- 1 cup water
- 8 eggs

Instructions

1. Add water into the instant pot and then place the eggs on top of the pot's rack or place in a steamer basket.

2. Cover pot with lid. Hit the manual button and set time to 5 minutes at high pressure.

3. Once cooking time is done, natural release the pressure for 5 more minutes and then quick release the pressure.

4. Transfer the hot eggs to cool ice water to halt cooking any more. Refrigerate for five minutes prior to peeling. Remove the shell of the hard boiled eggs.

13. BEST DAMN INSTANT POT EGG BITES

Preparation Time: 10 minutes | Cooking Time: 18 minutes | Serves: 7

Ingredients

- butter
- 4 large eggs
- 3oz gouda shredded cheese
- 1/4 cup fire roasted red peppers, diced
- 1/2 cup cottage cheese
- 1/4 cup heavy cream
- 1/2 cup spinach, fresh
- 1 teaspoon onion powder
- non-stick cooking spray
- 1/2 teaspoon salt

Instructions

1. Start by chopping red peppers and spinach. Place half tablespoon of butter into the Instant Pot and then press the sauté function. Once hot, place in red peppers and spinach and then sauté for one minute. Hit the cancel button.

2. Use non-stick cooking spray to spritz silicone egg bite mold and then scoop the spinach and red pepper mixture into each cup. Reserve.

3. Blend onion powder, eggs, salt, cottage cheese, gouda cheese and heavy cream in a blender for approximately 30 seconds.

4. Transfer the egg batter to each egg bite cup and fill to about 3/4. Once each cup is full, combine the batter with the red peppers and spinach with a spoon a little more.

5. Pour one cup of water into the Instant pot. Cover the egg bite mold with foil, then put on top of the trivet and place it inside the pot. Close the lid and seal. Set to steam for eight minutes. When time is up, natural release the pressure for ten minutes and then do a quick release to release the remaining pressure.

6. Take out the foil and allow to sit for about 5 to 10 minutes to cool prior to taking out and serving.

14. INSTANT POT EGG BITES

Preparation Time: 10 minutes | Cooking Time: 8 minutes | Serves: 7

Ingredients

Gruyere Egg Bites

- 5 eggs
- 1/4 teaspoon salt
- 2 ounces gruyere cheese, shredded or chopped into pieces
- 1/4 cup water

Egg white & red pepper egg bites

- 2 ounces feta cheese (approximately 1/3 cup crumbles)
- 8 egg whites (only)
- 1/4 cup water
- 1 small handful fresh spinach, chopped
- 1/4 cup sliced roasted red pepper (homemade or from a jar)
- 1/4 teaspoon salt

Pizza egg bites

- 1/4 teaspoon basil, dried
- 5 eggs
- 2 chopped green onions
- 2 tablespoons grated parmesan cheese
- 1/4 cup water
- 1/4 teaspoon salt
- 2 tablespoons finely chopped sundried tomatoes

Instructions

1. To prepare egg bites, mix cheese, eggs (or egg whites), salt, and water in a blender. Then blend at high speed until the resulting mixture is smooth.
2. In case you are adding other things to your egg bite, coat the silicone mold well (you can use spray oil) and then evenly drizzle the add-ins at the bottom of each well. Spread blended egg mixture on top and distribute it evenly among seven cups.
3. Add 1 cup of water into the instant pot and then put the handled trivet on top. Gently put the filled egg mold over the trivet. Close the lid and push steam release valve to the seal position. Set to cook for 8 minutes at high pressure.
4. Once cooking is done, release the pressure at least five minutes and then push steam release valve to the venting position to release the remaining pressure. (You can leave it longer to release naturally). Once floating valve in the lid has dropped, you can safely take out the lid.
5. Grab the handled trivet with oven mitts and take out mold with cooked egg bites. You can leave them to cool a bit for about 5 to 10 minutes, but be sure to serve them while still warm. The eggs are easier to remove from the mold when they're relatively hot.
6. Serve immediately. Transfer leftovers into an airtight container and then place in the refrigerator for up to four days.

15. HEALTHY INSTANT POT EGG ROLL BOWL RECIPE

Preparation Time: 10 minutes | Cooking Time: 10 minutes | Serves: 6-8

Ingredients

- 1 medium yellow onion, diced
- 1 teaspoon sesame oil
- 16oz (2 bags) of coleslaw mix
- 1/3 c. low sodium soy sauce
- 1 ½ lbs. lean ground turkey
- ½ c. chicken broth, low sodium
- 2 tablespoons minced garlic
- 1 tablespoon fresh ginger, minced
- Pepper and salt to taste
- Diced green onions for garnish if desired

Instructions

1. Hit the sauté button on the Instant Pot.

2. After the pot preheats, add garlic, yellow onion, sesame oil, and ground turkey. Then brown the meat until cooked. Hit cancel.

3. Pour in the remaining ingredients and do not stir.

4. Cover the pot with lid and ensure the valve is set to the sealing position. Set the time to 0 minutes at high pressure.

5. Once cooking cycle is done, do a quick release by gently pushing the valve to the venting position.

6. Mix and garnish, if preferred.

DESSERTS

1. INSTANT POT GERMAN CHOCOLATE CHEESECAKE

Preparation Time: 20 minutes | Cooking Time: 35 minutes | Serves: 10

Ingredients

For the cheesecake filling

- 2 tbsp. cocoa powder
- ½ cup sugar
- 2 large eggs, lukewarm
- 8 ounce (2 packages) cream cheese at lukewarm
- 1 tsp. vanilla extract
- 6 Oz bittersweet or German chocolate, melted and cooled till a little warm
- ¼ tsp. salt

For the Chocolate ganache

- ¾ cup semi-sweet chocolate chips
- ½ cup heavy cream

For the crust

- 3 tbsp. melted butter
- 1 cup chocolate wafer cookie crumbs

For the coconut pecan frosting

- ½ cup sliced pecans
- ¼ cup butter
- 2 egg yolks
- 2/3 cup flaked coconut

- ½ cup sugar
- 1 tsp vanilla
- ½ cup evaporated milk

Instructions

1. Use nonstick cooking spray to spritz a seven inch spring form pan. Alternatively, line parchment paper onto the bottom of the pan for easier removal of cake when done.

2. Mix melted butter and cookie crumbs together. Then spread evenly onto the bottom and one third up the sides of pan. Transfer into the freezer to set as you prepare the cheesecake filing.

3. Preparing the cheesecake filing: Use a handheld mixer on low speed to cream the cream cheese until it's very smooth. Scrape the bowl and combine once again.

4. Add cocoa powder, vanilla, salt, and sugar. Combine, scraping the sides at least once to incorporate everything well, until smooth.

5. Place in eggs and mix a bit with a hand mixer for about 5 seconds. Then mix all the way with a spatula.

6. Lastly, pour in the melted and cooled chocolate. Then mix with a spatula until incorporated.

7. Take out the pan from freezer and add the chocolate mixture until filled.

8. Pour 1 ½ cups water into the pressure cooker pot and then put in the trivet.

9. Gently lower the pan prepared onto trivet. Cover with the lid and then switch the pressure release valve to the sealed position. Cook for 35 minutes at high pressure.

10. Once pressure cooking is done, natural release pressure for 10 minutes and then release the remaining pressure.

11. Take out the pan from the pressure cooker and leave it to cool for ten minutes.

12. Gently remove spring form ring taking care not to break the crust.

13. Put the cheesecake into the fridge for a minimum of four hours to chill completely.

14. When cheesecake has cooled, make the coconut pecan frosting by mixing vanilla, butter, milk, sugar, and egg yolks in a small saucepan. Over medium heat, cook while stirring continuously for about 5 minutes until thickened.

15. Remove from the heat source, add pecans and coconut and stir vigorously until silky and well-incorporated.

16. Add the coconut pecan frosting on top of the cheesecake. Place the cheesecake back into the refrigerator.

17. To prepare the chocolate ganache: In a small heat safe bowl, put chocolate chips and reserve.

18. Place heavy cream in a small saucepan on top of medium heat and heat to a light simmer. Spread the hot cream atop the chocolate chips and then cover.

19. After three minutes elapse, remove the cover and then whip chocolate mixture vigorously until shiny and smooth.

20. Allow to cool to thicken a bit and then sprinkle atop the coconut pecan frosting. You can serve right away or refrigerate for a while to set the ganache. You can also make this cake one day ahead.

21. To have the best flavor and texture, allow to rest at lukewarm for approximately 1 hour prior to serving.

Cooking tips

- Ensure to use lukewarm cream cheese and eggs in order to have a smooth cream cheese filling.

- You need to plan ahead if not busy because cheesecakes normally taste better the second day.

- You can use the excess ganache to dunk strawberries.

- This cheesecake tastes best after resting for at least 1 hour at lukewarm when the ganache and frosting have soften a little.

- As you mix in eggs, it's advisable not to incorporate a lot of air into the batter. This is because overbeaten eggs usually make the batter to overflow during the cooking process.

2. AMAZING INSTANT POT KEY LIME CHEESECAKE

Preparation Time: 15 minutes | Cooking Time: 45 minutes | Serves: 6

Ingredients

For Cheesecake

- 2 eggs
- 16 oz. cream cheese softened to lukewarm
- ½ cup sugar
- 1 egg Yolk
- 2 teaspoon Vanilla
- 2 teaspoon Flour
- Zest of 1 Lime
- 3 tablespoon Key Lime Juice
- 2 tablespoon Heavy Whipping Cream

For crust

- 3 tablespoon melted butter
- 1 cup graham cracker crumbs

For topping

- 10 lime halves thinly sliced
- 2 tablespoon sugar

- ¾ cup heavy whipping cream
- Zest of 1 lime

Instructions

For the crust:

1. Use non-stick cooking spray to spritz a six inch springform pan and reserve. Use a fork to mix melted butter and graham cracker crumbs together in a small bowl. Then pour onto the bottom of the prepared pan, press firmly and reserve.

For the cheesecake filling:

1. Beat sugar, flour, vanilla, zest of one lime and cream cheese together using an electric mixer. Ensure you scrape the bottom and sides to prevent lumps and all ingredients are mixed well. Place in eggs, one by one, and then add the egg yolk. Beat till blended. Stir in whipping cream and key lime juice (you can use lime juice if it's hard to get key lime juice) until mixed. Spread on top of the crust. To remove large air bubbles, gently tap the pan on countertop several times.

Cooking:

1. Pour 1 ½ cups of water into the pressure cooker insert. Put trivet on the bottom of the insert. Spread a dry paper towel onto the springform pan and tightly warp with aluminum

foil. Use a sling to put the pan in the pressure cooker. Close with lid and then let to cook for 37 minutes at high pressure. After cooking is finished, natural release the pressure for about 18 minutes.

2. Gently take out from pressure cooker and then peel off the foil and paper towel. Transfer onto a wire rack to cool for ten minutes. Run a sharp paring knife around the edges between the pan and cheesecake. Allow to cool for about 20 to 30 minutes before releasing the edge of the springform pan. Then cover lightly and place in a refrigerator overnight.

Topping:

1. Take out the springform pan bottom from the cheesecake and then use a large spatula to transfer the cheesecake onto a serving platter. In a mixing bowl, put sugar and whipping cream and whip till stiff. Roll in zest of half of lime (reserve the other half of lime to zest all over the top for garnish).

2. Into a piping bag that has a large open star tip, add in whipping cream and then pipe over the instant pot cheesecake. Zest the other half of lime atop whipped cream and middle of cheesecake. Add lime slice halves around the cheesecake by gently sliding in the whipped cream. Ensure the slices are equidistance apart.

3. Chill while covered until serving.

3. INSTANT POT DEATH BY CHOCOLATE CHEESECAKE

Preparation Time: 10 minutes | Cooking Time: 35 minutes | Serves: 8

Ingredients

For crust:

- 20 double stuffed Oreo cookies

For filling:

- 2 eggs
- 2 packs cream cheese, lukewarm
- ½ cup heavy whipping cream
- ½ cup sour cream
- 2 tablespoons cocoa powder, unsweetened
- 4 oz. semi-sweet chocolate, melted
- 6 tablespoon sugar

- 1 teaspoon vanilla
- ½ cup chocolate chips

Ganache for topping

- ½ cup heavy whipping cream
- ½ cup chocolate chips

Instructions

1. To make the crust, add oreos into a food processor and then blend until they form crumbs.

2. Transfer the oreos into a six inch springform pan and then push down with a measuring cup or your hand.

3. Then freeze until the filling is ready.

4. To prepare the filling, begin with all lukewarm ingredients. In a large mixing bowl, add cream cheese and then mix on high until fluffy and light.

5. Pour in sugar and then stir until mixed.

6. Pour in sour cream and stir until mixed. Do not overmix.

7. Stir in vanilla, cocoa powder and melted chocolate until mixed.

8. Finally, add in the eggs, one by one and stir until fully incorporated.

9. Spread the filling over the prepared crust and then use tin foil to cover the top of the pan. You can also cover the pan's bottom if you want to.

10. Assemble the instant pot by adding a cup of water and then put the rivet ono the bottom of pot. You can form a sling with a piece of aluminum foil, then roll to form a long strip and place it over the trivet.

11. Put the pan into the pot and cover with lid to seal.

12. Cook for 35 minutes on high pressure.

13. Once 35 minutes elapse, natural release the pressure. Remove the lid, lift out the pan from the pot and put it on the counter to cool. You can leave the foil in place or remove it at this point. The contents will seem very jiggly and undercooked. After cooling completely, transfer to the refrigerator overnight.

14. After the cheesecake has set overnight, prepare the ganache by mixing cream and chocolate in a microwave safe bowl. Heat in microwave for 30 seconds intervals until most of the chocolate has melted. Mix until all choco has melted and thickens a bit. Spread over the cheesecake.

15. Serve.

4. DUMP CAKE IN THE INSTANT POT

Preparation Time: 10 minutes | Cooking Time: 25-28 minutes | Serves: 8

Ingredients

- 1 stick butter
- 1 to 21 oz. can apple pie filling
- Yellow cake mix, only ½ of the mix is needed

Instructions

1. Use cooking spray to lightly spritz a spring form pan. Spread evenly a can of pie filling onto the pan's bottom.

2. Drizzle the cake mix over the pie filling. Spread pats of butter all over the cake including at the middle. Pour one cup of water into the pot. Assemble the pan on the trivet and place it on the pot's bottom. Switch to high pressure for about 25 to 28 minutes. Once done, quick release the pressure and let to cool. Transfer the springform pan onto a plate. You can serve warm together with a dollop of whip cream or ice cream.

Tip: You can use different variations of cake mix and pie filling. Try out with blueberry pie filling or whole cake mix.

5. PUMPKIN CHEESECAKE IN THE INSTANT POT

Preparation Time: 10 minutes | Cooking Time: 35 to 40 minutes | Serves: 4

Ingredients

- 15 ounces pumpkin puree
- 2 packages 8 ounces each softened cream cheese,
- 2 teaspoons Pure Vanilla Extract
- 3/4 cup light brown sugar, firmly packed
- 1 1/2 teaspoons Pumpkin Pie Spice
- 2 cups vanilla wafer crumbs
- 3 eggs
- 2 tablespoons granulated sugar
- 1 tablespoon flour
- 3 tablespoons melted butter

Instructions

1. Into a 7 inch spring form pan, prepare the vanilla wafer crust by using crushed vanilla wafers and melted butter. Be sure wafers are fine and crumbled. You can use a ziplock bag to crumble with hand and crush in bag. Make sure you lightly spritz the pan's bottom.

2. Add sugar, butter and wafers and then combine thoroughly to form at the bottom.

3. Transfer the pan into a freezer as you prepare the cheesecake mixture.

4. To prepare the filling, use an electric mixer on medium speed to beat brown sugar and cream cheese in a large bowl until fluffy.

5. Add the eggs one by one while beating on low speed after each addition until well blended.

6. Add pumpkin pie spice, vanilla, flour and pumpkin and then beat until the resulting mixture is smooth. Spread into crust.

7. Transfer the mixture into the pan prepared and then put pan onto the trivet. Use foil to cover the pan.

8. Pour a cup and half of water into the instant pot.

9. Place the pan and trivet into the pot. Switch pot to high pressure manual for about 35 to 40 minutes. Once done, natural release the pressure.

10. Carefully take out the cheesecake and trivet. Let to cool.

11. Transfer into a fridge for four hours so as to set completely until when you are ready to serve.

6. INSTANT POT MASON JAR CAKE

Preparation Time: 8 minutes | Cooking Time: 22 minutes | Serves: 5

Ingredients

- 2 eggs, preferably lukewarm
- 2 cups Devil's Food Cake Mix, you can use Duncan Hines or any kind. Feel free to use any type of cake mix such as vanilla
- 2/3 cup water, lukewarm
- 2 ½ tablespoon cooking oil

Toppings

- Fresh Fruit of Choice
- Sprinkles
- Vanilla Frosting Duncan Hines
- Chocolate Frosting

Instructions

1. Put the inner pot into an 8 quart or 6 quart instant pot. Switch on the pot. Put trivet into the pot. Add two cups of water into the inner pot. Push the sauté button and then set on High. Heat the water until it begins to steam. Then press cancel after steaming. Doing this will speed up the process of bringing the pot on pressure. In the meantime, you can work on the cake batter.

2. Pick five to six mason canning jars of eight ounce each and coat them with cooking spray. Reserve.

3. Into a mixing bowl, place two cups of Duncan Hines Devil's food cake mix. Then add to the cake mix, water, eggs and cooking oil. Blend on medium speed for 2 minutes using a hand held blender until the batter is smooth.

4. Evenly divide the batter into 5 to 6 Jars. You can use five or six mason jars.

5. Be sure not to fill more than 2/3 of the jar. You will need to fill slightly less than 2/3 of the jar to leave enough room for cake to rise.

6. Use aluminum foil to cover the opening of the jars. Carefully transfer the jars into the pot onto the trivet. Place them close to each other. 6 jars of 8 ounce can easily fit on a trivet if using a six quart instant pot.

7. Cover the pot with the lid and ensure it is on the sealing position. Push the cake button and adjust to 22 minutes on normal cake and high pressure. In case your instant pot doesn't have the cake mode, you should adjust to the manual/pressure cooker setting and set on high pressure. The time is still the same.

8. When time elapses, natural release the pressure. You can open the lid after the safety valve has dropped. Carefully remove the mason jars and put them on the buffet. Take out the foil. Allow to rest until cool. The mason jar cakes will be ready after cooling.

9. When the cakes are cooled to room temperature, you can frost them with chocolate or vanilla frosting. Add some berries and sprinkles. Serve.

How to prepare jar cakes in four ounce jars

1. The process for four ounce does not change. Use about 10 to 12 canning jars of four ounce each. Add cake batter until 2/3 full, and then cover with foil. Carefully stack the jars. You can prepare about 10 to 12 jar cakes for four ounce.

2. You can make these four ounce cakes in jars for around 12 minutes. Natural release the pressure and then follow the instructions above for eight ounce jars.

How to use the leftover one cup cake mix

1. You can make use the leftover one cup of cake mix to prepare microwave cake.

2. Combine the 1 cup of cake mix with 1 tablespoon of cooking oil, 1 egg and 3 tablespoon of water. Then blend them together for about one minute until smooth. Coat a small 6x4 inch Pyrex bowl with grease and then add batter. Heat in microwave for about 2 minutes on high. Check for doneness in the center. If not done, heat in microwave for 30 seconds at a time until done. You will require about 2 ½ to 3 minutes to have a soft and spongy microwave cake.

7. INSTANT POT BLUEBERRY COBBLER

Preparation Time: 8 minutes | Cooking Time: 25 minutes | Serves: 5

Ingredients

- 1 teaspoon of cornstarch
- 2 cups of frozen blueberries
- ⅛ cup of lemon juice
- 1 teaspoon of vanilla extract
- 1 cup of sugar

Topping:

- 1 cup of milk
- 1 tablespoon of baking powder
- 2 cups of flour
- ¼ cup of melted butter
- ½ cup of sugar

Instructions

1. Assemble the filling in the Instant Pot. Add all the filling ingredients and combine thoroughly.

2. A burn error will be displayed in case you don't combine well and deglaze the bottom. This error means that the pan is too hot. Therefore, move the pan around and combine thoroughly.

3. Combine all your topping ingredients in a mixing bowl.

4. Spread them on top of the filling in an even layer.

5. Cover with the lid and move to the sealed position. Set the time to 25 minutes at manual high temperature.

6. Once done, natural release the pressure.

7. You can serve together with ice cream.

8. INSTANT POT CARAMEL APPLE DUMP CAKE

Preparation Time: 3 minutes | Cooking Time: 35 minutes | Serves: 8

Ingredients

- 1/4 cup caramel syrup
- 1 package 15 ounces yellow cake mix
- 1 can 21 ounces apple fruit filling
- 1/2 cup butter cut into thin slices

Instructions

1. Use nonstick cooking spray to spritz a glass bowl.

2. Onto the bottom, pour apple fruit filling.

3. Add caramel syrup on top and carefully combine with apples.

4. Add 3/4 of the dry cake mix on top. (you won't require the whole bag of cake mix)

5. Add a single layer on butter on top and ensure you cover all areas of the cake mix.

6. Put the trivet in the pot along with 1 cup of water.

7. Put the bowl onto the trivet.

8. Set the timer to 35 minutes on manual high pressure.

9. Quick release the pressure.

10. It's done if a toothpick comes out clean when inserted.

9. INSTANT POT CHOCOLATE FUDGE CAKE RECIPE

Preparation Time: 10 minutes | Cooking Time: 25 minutes | Serves: 4-7

Ingredients

- ¼ cup all-purpose flour
- ½ cup unsalted butter (1 stick)
- pinch of salt
- 2 large eggs
- ½ cup cocoa powder
- 1 cup granulated sugar

Instructions

1. Over low heat, melt one stick of butter in a sauce pan. When the butter melts, take out the pan from heat and add a pinch of salt, ¼ cup of flour, ½ cup of cocoa and 1 cup of sugar. Stir to mix all the ingredients. Add two eggs and then whisk the mixture thoroughly. The mix will seam separated and grainy in the beginning but continue whisking until shiny and smooth.

2. Use butter to coat 7 Hatrigo mini metal bowls or 4 – 4oz ramekins and then dust with flour. Shake to remove any excess flour. In case you are using silicone egg bites molds, you just need to butter them. Transfer batter into bowls until approximately 80% full.

3. Into the pot, add 1 cup of water and put the trivet into the pot. Stack ramekins at the top or put Hatrigo cake pan with mini bowls onto trivet. Cover the pot and set the timer to 33 minutes high pressure for Hatrigo mini bowls, 25 minutes at high pressure for 4 – 4oz Ramekins, and 25 minutes at high pressure for silicone egg bites tray.

4. When time elapses, quick release the steam by moving the valve to venting position. Open the lid when the pin drops. Let the cakes to sit for 1 minute before removing them. Cool the cakes for around ten minutes. Taking care of your hands because the bowls will still be warm, move a sharp paring knife along the margin and turn out cake on a small plate (no need to use a paring knife in case you used egg bites mold because they will easily pop out). Sprinkle powdered sugar on top and then serve with ice cream, berries or whipped cream.

10. PRESSURE COOKER KEY LIME PIE

Preparation Time: 10 minutes | Cooking Time: 15 minutes | Serves: 8

Ingredients

- 1/3 cup sour cream
- 3/4 cup graham-cracker crumbs, around 5 crackers
- 4 large egg yolks
- 3 tablespoons melted unsalted butter
- 14 ounces (1 can) sweetened condensed milk
- 1/2 cup fresh key lime juice
- 2 tablespoons grated key lime zest
- 1 tablespoon sugar

Instructions

Graham cracker crust

1. Use a non-stick spray to coat a 7 inch springform pan.

2. Mix sugar, butter and graham cracker crumbs in a small bowl. Evenly spread at the bottom and up the side of pan. Transfer into a freezer for ten minutes.

Filling

1. Beat egg yolks in a large mixing bowl until light yellow. Slowly beat in the sweetened condensed milk until thickened. Slowly add the lime juice and then beat until smooth. Mix in zest and sour cream. Transfer the batter into springform pan over the crust. Use aluminum foil to cover the top of the springform pan.

2. Add one cup of water into the instant pot and then put trivet at the bottom. Carefully center the filled pan onto a foil sling and then place it inside the pot. Roll down the foil sling to prevent it from interfering with the lid.

3. Close the pot with the lid and then set to high pressure for 15 minutes. When time's up, switch off the cooker. Natural release the pressure for 10 minutes and then quick release any remaining pressure. Once the valve drops, gently remove the lid. Take out the pie and check whether the center is set. If not set, let to cook for 5 more minutes.

4. Transfer springform pan onto a wire rack to cool. Take out the aluminum foil. Once the pie has cooled, cover with plastic wrap and chill for at least 4 hours. If desired, you can serve together with whipped cream.

Notes: You can use ¼ cup lime juice and ¼ cup fresh lemon juice in place of key limes. You can form a sling with a 20 inch piece of aluminum foil by folding 3 times length wise.

11. CHOCOLATE FUDGE CAKE

Preparation Time: 20 minutes | Cooking Time: 35 minutes | Serves: 6-8

Ingredients

- Vanilla ice cream for serving
- 5 tablespoons melted unsalted butter and more for greasing
- 1/2 teaspoon pure vanilla extract
- 1/4 cup unsweetened cocoa powder and more for dusting
- 1 cup all-purpose flour
- 1/4 teaspoon kosher salt
- 1 teaspoon baking powder
- 2 large eggs
- 8 ounces chocolate chips, semisweet
- 1 espresso (or 1 tablespoon of instant espresso powder combined with 2 tablespoons of boiling water)
- 1 cup granulated sugar

Instructions

1. Use butter to coat a 7-inch springform pan.

2. Whisk together baking powder, flour, salt and cocoa powder in a small bowl.

3. Whisk together espresso, eggs, vanilla, sugar, and melted butter in a medium bowl. Carefully whisk dry mixture into wet mixture. Roll in chocolate chips. Transfer the mixture to the pan prepared and then cover with aluminum foil.

4. Into the instant pot, add 1 1/4 cup water and then put springform pan over the steam rack. Lower the pan into pot using the handles. Cover with the lid and then move the valve to the sealing position. Push the pressure cook button and set time to 35 minutes at high pressure.

5. Natural release the steam release for 15 minutes and then move valve to the venting to quick-release the remaining steam. Gently take out the lid and then remove the pan using steam rack handles. Place onto a cooling rack, take out the foil and leave to cool completely.

6. To serve, take out the pan sides, drizzle cocoa powder onto cake and then slice into wedges. You can serve together with scoops of vanilla ice cream.

12. INSTANT POT CHEESECAKE

Preparation Time: 10 minutes | Cooking Time: 35 minutes | Serves: 6-8

Ingredients

For the crust

- Pinch of salt
- Cooking spray for the pan
- 3 tablespoon melted butter
- 1 c. crushed graham crackers

For the cheesecake

- 2 eggs
- 16 oz. (2 blocks) softened cream cheese
- 1 tablespoon all-purpose flour
- 1/4 c. light brown sugar
- 1/2 c. granulated sugar
- 1/4 c. sour cream
- 1/4 teaspoon kosher salt
- 1 teaspoon pure vanilla extract
- Sliced strawberries for garnish
- Cool whip for garnish

Directions

1. Making the crust: Use cooking spray to coat a 6" springform pan. Mix salt, melted butter and graham cracker crumbs in a medium bowl. Combine until the mixture has the texture of wet sand. Evenly spread at the pan's bottom and up the side. Place in a freezer for 20 minutes.

2. Making cheesecake: Use a hand mixer to beat flour, sour cream, cream cheese, and sugars in a large bowl until fluffy and light. Add salt and vanilla and then beat until mixed. Add the eggs, one by one and then beat until blended. Avoid overmixing. Transfer batter into springform pan over the crust.

3. Into the instant pot, add 1½ cups of water and then put the trivet at the bottom. Roll a large piece of foil (of around 18 inches) into thirds to form a long "sling". Then place into the pot. Place springform pan on top and then roll the sling.

4. Cover the pot with the lid, then set to high pressure for 35 minutes. Natural release the pressure. Use the sling to take out cheesecake from pot and then transfer to cool on a wire rack a minimum of 1 hour.

5. Cover the springform pan with foil and then place in fridge for four hours or up to overnight. Top with cool whip and then stud with sliced strawberries. Serve.

CONCLUSION

By now you should have no doubts about how easy and simple to cook food in an instant pot. Some of the instant pot recipes are super simple to make and hence, you shouldn't feel nervous if this is your first time to cook with an instant pot. In addition, the ingredients in each recipe are simple to find since they are available in grocery stores and local supermarkets near your residence. All of the recipes are very easy to follow and some offer replacements for ingredients that probably might be difficult to find in grocery stores.

Anything good for your heart is perfect for your taste buds as well. In this cookbook, the recipes will show you that you don't have to sacrifice flavor in order to enjoy healthy foods. Choosing a variety of foods is one way to have a healthy diet. Variety is very important because no food has all the essential nutrients required by your body. A healthy eating plan emphasizes on eating lean meats, egg, poultry, beans, fish, nuts, whole grains, vegetables, fruits and low-fat milk products. In addition, you should limit intake of sodium, added sugar, trans fat and saturated fat. This cookbook can help you in your healthy eating plan because it contains different types of foods groups such as seafood and poultry, eggs and vegetables, beef and pork and soups and stews categories. In addition, the recipes in the book are designed to lend you a satisfying amount and still remain within your calorie estimates.

This cookbook will help you discover and taste the real possibilities of your new instant pot. You will be astonished how simple and quick the recipes are to make. I'm confident that you will get to know that cooking with your new instant pot is fast, simple and fun. I hope you will fall in love with the recipes in this cookbook and often make them for your guests and during special occasions like family gatherings and parties.

I would like to thank all readers in advance who will/have read and try/tried out the recipes in this book and I hope you will enjoy these simple recipes. Don't keep great things for yourself, pass the recipes to your colleagues, friends and relatives.

Made in United States
North Haven, CT
28 December 2021

13783148R00063